A THESAURUS
of Spanish Idioms
and EVERYDAY LANGUAGE

By

LAWRENCE K. BROWN

FREDERICK UNGAR PUBLISHING CO.

NEW YORK

1520 GRANT

03

Printed by arrangement with Marcel Rodd, Inc.

Eighth Printing, 1980

ISBN 0-8044-0059-8 (cloth)
ISBN 0-8044-6059-0 (paper)

Library of Congress Catalog Card No. 54-7417

HOW TO USE THIS BOOK

The material is divided into seven parts. Parts I through IV, and Part VII, consist of Spanish idioms, expressions, etc., usable and readily understood, both for meaning and flavor, throughout Spanish America and Spain. Parts V and VI are devoted to Spanish America, exclusively; but in each case where an entry is in current use and popular in the mother country, we have noted alongside it—(*Sp.*).

The author takes this opportunity of requesting correspondence from students, scholars, and natives of Spain and our Spanish-American neighbor republics, pointing to any error that may have inadvertently crept into the text.

ABBREVIATIONS

s.o.—said of
sarc.—sarcastic
fig.—figurative (ly)
lit.—literal (ly)
finan.—financial

ref.—referring
fam.—familiar
expr.—expression
inf.—influence
ex. pol.—expression of politeness

It should be pointed out to the reader that we have purposely omitted in the text the innumerable two- and three-word phrases, e.g., *por lo tanto* (for that reason); *por degracia* (unfortunately); *desde luego* (right away; of course); *mientras tanto* (meanwhile); *sin embargo* (however); *no obstante* (notwithstanding); *por eso* (therefore); *por fin* (finally); *cuanto antes* (as soon as possible); *con tal que* (provided); *a menos que* (unless); *en seguida* (immediately), etc., of which not only elementary Spanish is made up, but all European languages. True enough, many of these might be regarded as fundamentally idiomatic. But we felt obliged to discipline ourselves, not only regarding the dimensions of this first edition, but also the nature of the work: it seemed to us that were we to include every short ejaculation, emphatic expression, or colloquial word, our compilation would quickly degenerate into a "vocabulary."

CONTENTS

FOREWORD

It is well known that students of Spanish frequently become discouraged at their seemingly slow progress in coping with the language as it is currently spoken by nationals of the Spanish-speaking countries. What they mostly complain of, after they have grasped a *grammar-book* knowledge of the language, is their inability to cope with *colloquial* Spanish—those countless peculiar expressions that are incomprehensible to their alien ears and which, unfortunately, have not been included in their basic school or college training.

What the author has done in the pages that follow is to place at the disposal of the reader about eight hundred of what he has found to be the most current, useful and popular idioms, colloquialisms, familiar expressions, humorous phrases, slang expressions, proverbs, axioms, adages, etc., that find their way into the everyday conversation of the average Spaniard and Spanish-American. Each entry is given in Spanish and in English, together with a practical example of its everyday usage, in both languages.

The compilation was realized in the following way:

Some seven years ago the author first began jotting down various expressions, idioms, etc., that he heard in the general run-of-the-mill type of daily conversation between nationals of the Spanish-speaking countries. These were typed on an index card with the following information: *idiom; English equivalent; name of person who ventured same;* and *country of which he was a national.* After fifty or more of these cards had been collected, and each had been checked by other nationals of the country under which it had been classified, the next step was to inquire of some ten or fifteen nationals of *another* country to determine if the term was in current use in *their* particular country. Naturally, new idioms were recorded, and those that stood the test of hashing and rehashing have found their respective place in this book in one of the seven sections. Those that were found to be archaic were discarded. Each remaining entry, then, has been checked *at least* fifteen times against *one individual country,* and, further, it has been checked against two hundred or more nationals from the seventeen Spanish-speaking republics, and Spain, represented in this book. Fifty per cent of those who assisted in the checking were people you would meet in everyday walks of life—shop girls, secretaries, sales-people, exchange students, and so on. The other fifty per cent were consular officials, doctors, lawyers, business-men, and so on. These entries, then, have been compiled from the ranks of *contemporary* individuals, and not from reference books or dictionaries.

It is hoped that the material will serve the following purposes:

(1) Acquaint the ambitious student and tourist with a popular style of everyday Spanish.

(2) Afford him an outlet into Spanish for many of his *own* vernacular and pet colloquial expressions, so many of which *do* exist in Spanish.

(3) Help nationals of the *Spanish-speaking* countries, who are studying English, to find a popular English equivalent for *their* idioms, colloquialisms, etc.

Needless to say, there are *many* expressions in colloquial and idiomatic English that do *not* exist in Spanish, simply because the Latin mind is in most ways *far* different from our own. For example, our institution of "going steady" does not exist to the Spanish way of thinking or living. A boy does not "go steady" with a girl in Spanish America or Spain. He either knows her as a *conocida* (acquaintance), or they are *comprometidos* (engaged).

This book makes no pretense at being complete. The fact that only one page may be devoted, for example, to Bolivia, and six pages to Mexico, does not indicate that Bolivia is lacking in col-loquialisms, but rather that the author was not able at this writing to amass a larger number of worth-while entries for this particular country.

It must be taken into consideration that, at times, an *exact* equivalent for a given Spanish term is *impossible* to render in the English language. An idiomatic, colloquial or slang expres-sion cannot always be broken down into its *absolute* meaning. Much depends on the particular circumstance in which the expres-sion is used, as there are always slight shades of difference in meaning, depending on each individual case. Frequently, there *is* no equivalent in our language that *we* could comprehend.

We assure the reader that our equivalents, from the Spanish to the English, or vice versa, are authentic in *flavor* and are perfectly acceptable for all general purposes; we do not, however, vouch for any degree of *literal* accuracy. Needless to say literal translations of idioms from one language to another are not only impossible, but, from the very nature of idioms, useless.

Parts II and IV have a TABLE OF CONVERSIONS. It is suggested that the reader, if he is interested in one particular country's way of rendering, more colloquially, a *given* Spanish idiom, expression, etc., consult these tables. Naturally, these tables are not foolproof, nor are they complete. They have been set up to show what type of research *could* be done by an ambitious student.

Many expressions are popular only in certain regions or countries, outside of which they remain completely unknown. With this in mind, we have devoted a section to colloquialisms, etc., peculiar to *Individual Spanish-American Republics,* and a section to colloquialisms, etc., peculiar to *Several Spanish-American Republics, Collectively*—attempting to exclude from these as many *regionalisms* as possible, and thus set down in writing only those expressions, etc., that are peculiar to a country *as a whole.*

For the most part, colloquialisms are uttered quickly, and frequently with little regard for the rules that govern text-book Spanish grammar. Long-drawn-out sentences hardly play a part in this colorful type of Spanish. The author has endeavored to offer a *practical* example of those entries in Parts V and VI in the same shortened style in which they appear most commonly in the everyday language of each *individual* country treated in the text. Consequently many repetitions (e.g., a predominance of the third person singular) may be encountered in these sections. When a short example is given in *any* section, for that matter, it has been done so deliberately to indicate that the entry cannot be extended without ruining its colloquial value. For example, the Mexican colloquialism PELAR GALLO is used only in the third person singular of the past tense. It is never extended beyond *peló gallo* (He flew the coop). The individual circumstances in which colloquialisms are used will carry their meaning without resorting to involved sentences. Make your constructions short and snappy if you want to retain their true value and preserve their colloquial flavor, and thus embellish your Spanish with the colorful sayings and expressions that predominate in the everyday language of your Spanish-speaking friends.

Since it was not possible, at the present writing, to include a section solely devoted to Spain, a thorough review of the entire material was made from the SPANISH point of view. Parts I, II, III, IV and VII, in their entirety, have proved through exhaustive tests to be acceptable and in popular use in the mother country. The same is true of only those entries in Parts V and VI that are preceded by (*Sp.*).

A word to the "loísta" and "leísta" factions

We are using *lo* (appended to the infinitive) on those entries that require a DIRECT object pronoun, and *le* on those requiring an INDIRECT object pronoun. For the sake of euphony, as well as clarity in some instances, a few entries carry *a uno* placed immediately after the infinitive, instead of (or together with) the appended pronoun.

L. K. B.

ACKNOWLEDGMENTS

The writer wishes to express his appreciation to the following people—and those countless others whose special request it was to remain unknown—who generously gave of their time and knowledge of contemporary Spanish in checking the conclusions and offering valuable suggestions, changes and additions:

CONSULAR OFFICIALS IN LOS ANGELES

Dr. Emilio Lascano Tegui, former Consul of Argentina; Sr. Juan M. Gutiérrez, Acting Consul of Argentina; Sr. Walter Montenegro, Consul of Bolivia; Dr. Manuel María Muñoz O., former Consul of Colombia; Sr. Guillermo Restrepo, Acting Consul of Colombia, and Sr. Rafael Escallón, Chancellor; Sr. Juan Pradenas M., Consul General of Chile, and Sres. Carlos Grant Benavente and Miguel Padilla, Consuls; Colonel Fernando Flores B., Consul General of Costa Rica, and Sr. Jorge Maroto B., Consul; Dr. Oscar Presmanes, Consul of Cuba; Dr. José A. Baquero, former Consul of Ecuador; Sr. Ramón González Montalvo, Consul of El Salvador, and Sr. J. Francisco Alvarenga, Chancellor; Dr. Julio C. Quintana V., Consul of Nicaragua, and Sr. Edgar Peñalba, Honorary Vice Consul; Sr. Felipe Rotalde, Consul of Peru.

Sr. Fernando García, friend of long standing and former instructor of foreign languages at Hollywood Military Academy, Los Angeles; Mr. Addison Durland, Latin-American Advisor of the Motion Picture Producers and Distributors of America, Inc.; Sr. Alberto Soria, of Argentina; Sr. Alberto Anaya and family, of Colombia; Sr. Julio Abadía, of Colombia; Sr. Luis Zeledón and family, of Costa Rica; Sta. Carmen Roldán, Professor of Spanish and Literature in "Colegio Superior de Señoritas, San José, Costa Rica; Sta. Rita Rozada of Cuba, and friend of long standing; Sra. Josephine Casanova Jiménez, of Cuba; Dr. Eduardo Orbe, former professor of Latin-American Civilization at the University of Southern California; Sra. James Gillespie and family, of Ecuador; Stas. Alicia Montalvo and Mimi Aguilar, of El Salvador; Sras. Elvira Lavalle and Estela Cheesman, of Guatemala; Sra. Aida Sevilla, of Honduras; Sr. A. A. Loyo, of the Loyo School of Spanish and Spanish Stenography, Los Angeles; Mrs. Frances Purtell, of the Purtell School of Spanish, Los Angeles; Sr. Juan José Montesinos, of Mexico City; Sr. Edmondo Alvarez, Mexican and friend of long standing; Sr. Oscar Martín Jiménez, of University High School, West Los Angeles; Sr. Juan B. Chevalier, of Panama; Sr. Victor Ortiz A., instructor in the Paraguayan grade schools; Sres. Reynaldo Luza and Alberto Rondón, of Peru; Sr. Marcelino Fernández, of Uruguay; Sr. Jesús M. Sánchez C., of Venezuela.

PART I

BASIC UNIVERSAL ELEMENTARY IDIOMS

PART I

BASIC UNIVERSAL ELEMENTARY IDIOMS

130 Idioms, Expressions, and Phrases, Common to All Spanish-Speaking People Everywhere. This First List is Indispensable to an Elementary Speaking and Reading Knowledge of the Spanish Language.

A continuación—below; as follows.

Los puntos principales de su discurso los publicamos a continuación.
Below, we reveal the principal points of his speech.

A diestra y siniestra—right and left.

Estaba dando golpes a diestra y siniestra.
He was throwing punches right and left.

A fin de cuentas—in the final analysis.

A fin de cuentas, no pudimos hacer nada.
In the final analysis, we could do nothing.

A fines de—late in; towards the end of (week, month, year, etc.).

A fines de mayo, le escribí una carta.
Towards the end of May I wrote you a letter.

A la larga—in the long run.

A la larga, ganaremos más dinero.
In the long run, we'll make more money.

[17]

A lo lejos—in the distance.

A lo lejos se puede ver la Ciudad de México.
Mexico City can be seen in the distance.

A más no poder—to the utmost; to the limit; full blast; to beat the band.

La (*or* el) radio tocaba a más no poder.
The radio was playing full blast.

A más tardar—at the latest.

Tendremos que salir el 15 de abril, a más tardar.
We shall have to leave April 15th, at the latest.

A mediados de—about the middle of (week, month, year, etc.).

Espero llegar a Buenos Aires a mediados de junio.
I hope to arrive in Buenos Aires about the middle of June.

A principios de—early in; about the first part of (week, month, year, etc.).

A principios del mes saldremos para La Paz.
We shall leave for La Paz about the first part of the month.

A propósito—by the way; apropos; speaking of . . .

(1) A propósito, ¿qué va a hacer esta noche?
By the way, what are you going to do tonight?

(2) A propósito de tu carta, la encuentro muy interesante.
Speaking of your letter, I find it very interesting.

A ver—Let's see.

(1) Used as a complete thought.

(2) A ver si tengo el dinero.
Let's see if I have the money.

Al fin y al cabo—after all.

Al fin y al cabo, ¿qué se puede hacer?
After all, what can be done?

Al parecer—to all appearances; apparently; seemingly.

Al parecer, es un hombre muy rico.
To all appearances, he is a rich man.

Al pie de la letra—word for word; literally; exactly.

Sus obras son difíciles de traducir al pie de la letra.
His works are difficult to translate literally.

Andar de mal en peor—to go from bad to worse.

Mis negocios andan de mal en peor.
My business is going from bad to worse.

Camino de—on the road to; on the way to.

Mañana estaremos camino de Nueva York.
Tomorrow we shall be on our way to New York.

Como de costumbre—as usual.

Estaba borracho, como de costumbre.
He was drunk, as usual.

¡Con razón!—No wonder!

(1) Used as a complete thought.

(2) ¡Con razón estás enfermo!
No wonder you are sick!

Contar con—to count, or rely, on; to have.

Nuestra biblioteca cuenta con una sección española muy buena.
Our library has a very good Spanish section.

Costar mucho trabajo—to be very difficult; to take a lot of effort in doing.

Cuesta mucho trabajo escribir un libro.
It takes a lot of effort to write a book.

Cueste lo que cueste (or **costare**)—Regardless of the cost; cost what it may (*fig. & lit.*).

Cueste lo que cueste, voy a comprar esa casa.
Regardless of the cost, I am going to buy that house.

¡Cuidado con . . . !—Be careful of . . . !

¡Cuidado con el perro!
Be careful of the dog!

Cumplir (con) su palabra—to keep, or to be true to, one's word.

Juan es muchacho que siempre cumple (con) su palabra.
John is a boy who always keeps his word.

Dar de comer—to feed.

Su mamá le ha dado de comer.
His mother has fed him.

Dar en qué pensar—to give food for thought.

Lo que hoy he leído en los periódicos me da mucho en qué pensar.
What I have today read in the newspapers gives me quite a little food for thought.

Dar parte de que—to report; to make a report.

El teniente quiere dar parte de que el enemigo ha atacado el puente.
The lieutenant wishes to report that the enemy has attacked the bridge.

[20]

Dar tiempo al tiempo—to bide one's time.

Hay que dar(le) tiempo al tiempo.
One should bide his time.

Darle lo mismo—to be all the same to one; not to make any difference to one.

Me da lo mismo.
It's all the same to me; it makes no difference to me.

Darse cuenta de que—to realize; to notice.

(1) Me dí cuenta de que la niña estaba llorando.
I noticed that the girl was crying.

(2) Tú no te das cuenta de las muchas dificultades que la cosa presenta.
You do not realize the many difficulties that the thing presents.

Darse por ofendido—to take offense; to become offended.

Cuando no le hablamos, se dió por ofendido.
When we didn't speak to him he became offended.

Darse por vencido—to give up; to acknowledge defeat.

El enemigo no se dará por vencido.
The enemy will not acknowledge defeat.

Dárselas de *plus noun*—to claim, or profess, to be.

Nunca me las dí de profeta.
I never claimed to be a prophet.

De buena gana—willingly; gladly.

Lo haremos de buena gana.
We shall do it willingly.

[21]

De buenas a primeras—on the spur of the moment; without reflection.

No me gusta tomar resoluciones de buenas a primeras.
I do not like to make decisions on the spur of the moment.

De cabo a rabo—from beginning to end.

He leído tu carta de cabo a rabo.
I have read your letter from beginning to end.

De lo lindo—wonderfully; perfectly.

Anoche nos divertimos de lo lindo.
Last night we had a wonderful time.

De mala gana—unwillingly.

Lo hicieron, pero de muy mala gana.
They did it, but very unwillingly.

De nada (or **por nada**)—Don't mention it. You are welcome. (*ex. pol.*)

¡De ninguna manera!—I should say not! Nothing of the sort! Under no circumstances!

De repuesto—extra; spare.

Siempre llevamos dos llantas de repuesto.
We always carry two spare tires.

De todos modos—at any rate; anyhow; in any event.

De todos modos nos veremos mañana.
At any rate, we'll see each other tomorrow.

De vez en cuando—from time to time.

Las muchachas vienen a visitarnos de vez en cuando.
The girls come to visit us from time to time.

[22]

Dentro de poco—within a short time.

Estarán aquí dentro de poco.
They will be here within a short time.

Dicho y hecho—sure enough; as was expected; no sooner said than done.

Le dije que Juan llegaría, y dicho y hecho él apareció.
I told him that John would come, and sure enough he showed up.

Echar al correo—to mail; to post.

Esta carta está lista para echarla al correo.
This letter is ready to be mailed.

Echar a perder—to ruin, or spoil.

No eches a perder tu traje nuevo.
Don't ruin your new suit.

Echar de menos—to miss; to feel the absence of.

Mucho echo de menos a mi amigo, Antonio.
I miss my friend, Anthony, very much.

En el fondo—at heart; in substance.

En el fondo, son individuos bien intencionados.
At heart they are well-meaning people.

En la actualidad—at the present time.

En la actualidad hay racionamiento de muchas cosas.
At the present time there is rationing of many things.

En otros términos—in other words.

En otros términos, todo está concluido.
In other words the whole thing is finished.

[23]

En pleno día—in broad daylight.

Robaron a la pobre muchacha en pleno día.
They robbed the poor girl in broad daylight.

En punto—on the dot; sharp. (*ref. to time*)

Llegaron a las cinco en punto.
They arrived at five o'clock sharp.

¿En qué puedo servirle?—What can I do for you? (*ex. pol.*)

En vigor—in force.

Éstas son las leyes que ya están en vigor.
These are the laws that are now in force.

¡Eso es!—That's it! That's right!

¡Eso mismo!—That's it exactly! The very thing!

Estar al corriente (or **al tanto**) **de**—to be posted, informed, or
up to date, on.

Si ustedes quieren estar al corriente (*or* al tanto) de lo que
está pasando, lean los periódicos.
If you want to be up to date on what is happening, read the
newspapers.

Estar de acuerdo—to agree; to be in accordance.

No estamos de acuerdo con usted.
We do not agree with you.

Estar de prisa—to be in a hurry.

Estoy de prisa.
I am in a hurry.

[24]

Estar de vuelta (or **regreso**)—to be back; to have returned.

Creo que estará de vuelta (*or* regreso) dentro de poco.
I think he will be back within a short time.

Estar de vacaciones—to be on (one's) vacation.

Todos mis amigos están de vacaciones.
All my friends are on (their) vacation.

Faltar al respeto a—to show no respect for; to treat disrespectfully.

No faltes al respeto a tu mamá.
Don't treat your mother disrespectfully.

Faltar a su palabra—to break one's word; not to keep one's word.

Prometió estar aquí a las seis en punto, pero faltó a su palabra.
He promised to be here at six o'clock sharp, but he didn't keep his word.

Faltar poco para que *plus imperfect subjunctive*—to come near to . . . to almost . . .

Poco faltó para que se cayera.
He came near falling.

Fuera de broma—all kidding, or joking, aside.

Fuera de broma, te voy a decir una cosa.
All kidding aside, I'm going to tell you something.

Ganar(se) la vida—to earn a living, or livelihood.

Estos muchachos venden periódicos para ganarse la vida.
These boys sell newspapers in order to earn a living.

[25]

Habérselas con—to answer to (in the sense of having to contend with, or account to).

Si lo hace, se las tendrá que haber con su papá.
If you do it, you'll have your father to answer to.

Hacer caso de—to pay attention to; to heed.

No hizo caso de lo que le dijimos.
He paid no attention to what we told him.

Hacer escala en—to make a stop at; to dock at. (*s.o. boats only*)

El vapor hace escala en San Francisco.
The steamship makes a stop at San Francisco.

Hacer falta *plus indirect object*—to lack; to be in need of.

Lo que (a usted) le hace falta es la práctica.
What you are in need of is practice.

Hacer un papel—to play a part, or rôle.

El artista hizo un papel muy importante en la película.
The artist played a very important part in the film.

Hacer un viaje—to take a trip.

Pensamos hacer un viaje a Cuba en verano.
This summer we intend to take a trip to Cuba.

Hacerse entender—to make one's self understood.

Hablo español bastante bien para hacerme entender.
I speak Spanish well enough to make myself understood.

Ir a medias—to go halves; to go 50-50.

Si compramos el automóvil, vamos a medias.
If we buy the automobile, let's go 50-50.

[26]

Ir de compras—to go shopping.

Se fueron de compras.
They went shopping.

Ir de vacaciones—to go on (one's) vacation.

¿Cuando vas a ir de vacaciones?
When are you going on (your) vacation?

Llegar a ser—to become; to get to be.

Llegó a ser el cirujano más destacado de la ciudad.
He got to be the most outstanding surgeon in the city.

Llevarse bien (or **mal**) **con uno**—to get along well (or badly) with one.

El empleado no se lleva muy bien con su jefe.
The employee does not get along very well with his boss.

Más acá de—on this side of; before you get to . . .

La biblioteca queda más acá de Broadway.
The library is on this side of (*or* before you get to) Broadway.

Más allá de—on the other side of; beyond.

Más allá de las montañas hay un valle hermoso.
Beyond the mountains is a beautiful valley.

No cabe duda—There's no question, or doubt, about it; there's no room for doubt.

(1) Used as a complete thought, as in the above phrase.

(2) No cabe duda de que María es la mejor de su clase.
There's no doubt about it that Mary is the best in her class.

[27]

(No) caer bien *plus indirect object*—(1)—(not) to fit well; (not) to be becoming. (2)—not to agree with (as food or drink).

(1) Ese traje le cae muy bien.
    That suit is very becoming to you.

(2) La bebida no me cae bien.
    Drinking doesn't agree with me.

(No) darse por entendido—(not) to take the hint: *used mostly in the negative.*

No se dió por entendido.
He didn't take the hint.

No hay de qué (or No hay por qué)—Don't mention it. You're welcome. (*ex. pol.*)

No poder con—not to be able to manage, or handle; to be too much for one.

No podemos con la niña.
We cannot manage the child (She is too much for us).

No poder más—to be all played out; to be exhausted; to be all in.

No puedo más.
I'm all played out.

No poder menos que (or de) *plus infinitive*—not to be able to help but . . .

El profesor no pudo menos que (*or* de) reír.
The teacher couldn't help but laugh.

No tenga usted cuidado—Don't worry about; Forget it. (*ex. pol.*)

No tengo cómo pagarle—I don't know how to repay you for your kindness. (*ex. pol.*)

[28]

Para (or **por**) **siempre jamás**—forever and ever.
(1) Used as a complete thought.
(2) Desearíamos vivir aquí para (*or* por) siempre jamás.
We should like to live here forever and ever.

Pasar las vacaciones—to spend one's vacation.

Este año mi amigo y yo pasaremos las vacaciones en Sud
América.
This year my friend and I will spend our vacation in South
America.

Pasar revista a—to review; to inspect.

El coronel pasó revista a las tropas.
The colonel reviewed the troops.

Pasar(se) sin—to do without; to get along without.

Hoy día tenemos que pasar(nos) sin muchas cosas.
Nowadays we have to get along without many things.

Pedir prestado—to borrow.

Paquita me pidió prestado un dólar.
Fanny borrowed a dollar from me.

Poner al corriente—to keep up to date, or posted; to inform.

No deje de ponernos al corriente de los negocios que pudiesen
presentarse.
Don't fail to keep us posted on any matters that might arise.

[29]

Por las buenas o por las malas—(1) willingly or by force.
(2) by hook or crook.

(1) Vendrás conmigo por las buenas o por las malas.
You will come with me either willingly or by force.

(2) Me apoderaré del dinero por las buenas o por las malas.
I will get possession of the money by hook or crook.

Por lo pronto—for the time being.

Por lo pronto no podemos decirle nada.
For the time being we cannot tell you anything.

Por regla general—as a general rule.

Por regla general nos acostamos temprano.
As a general rule we go to bed early.

Por si acaso *plus indicative mood*—if by chance; just in case.

Por si acaso no estoy cuando vuelvas, deja un recado.
If by chance I am not in when you return, leave a message.

Por término medio—on an average.

Por término medio leemos dos libros por semana.
We read on an average two books a week.

Pronunciar un discurso—to make a speech.

Espero que el presidente no pronuncie un discurso muy largo.
I hope the chairman doesn't make a long speech.

¿Puedo servirle en algo?—Can I do something for you? (*ex. pol.*)

¿Qué le parece?—What do you think of (it)?

(1) Used as a complete thought, as in the above phrase.

(2) ¿Qué le parece mi novia?
What do you think of my girl-friend?

[30]

¿Qué sé yo?—How should I know?

Pepe: —¿Cuándo va a volver tu papá?
Juan: —¿Qué sé yo?

Joe: When is your father going to return?
John: How should I know?

Quedar en *plus infinitive*—to agree to . . .

Quedó en verme mañana.
He agreed to see me tomorrow.

Quedarse con—to keep (in the sense of taking or retaining).

Me quedo con éste.
I'll take this one.

Querer decir—to mean; to mean to say.

¿Qué quiere decir este modismo?
What does this idiom mean?

Saber de memoria—to know by heart.

Lo saben de memoria.
They know it by heart.

Sea como fuere—Be that as it may.

Sea como fuere, no le puedo pagar más dinero.
Be that as it may, I cannot pay you more money.

Sea lo que sea—*Same as above.*

Si mal no recuerdo—If I remember correctly.

Si mal no recuerdo, hoy es el día de pago.
If I remember correctly, today is pay-day.

[31]

Sin ton ni son—without rhyme or reason.

Lo hizo sin ton ni son.
He did it without rhyme or reason.

(NOTE: *sin son ni ton,* as an alternative, is often heard
in Spain and some parts of Spanish America)

Tal para cual—two of a kind (*sarc.*); tit for tat.

Tarde o temprano—sooner or later.

Tarde o temprano verás que no te he aconsejado mal.
Sooner or later you'll see that I have not ill-advised you.

Tener al corriente—to keep up to date, or posted; to inform.

Yo le tendré al corriente de lo que ocurra.
I'll keep you up to date on what happens.

Tener . . . años—to be . . . years old.

Margarita tiene quince años, y yo tengo doce.
Margaret is fifteen years old, and I am twelve.

Tener cuidado—to take care; to be careful.

Te ruego tener cuidado con todo lo que hagas.
I beg of you to be careful of everything you do.

Tener ganas de *plus infinitive*—to feel like . . .

Tengo ganas de hacer un viaje por la América del Sur.
I feel like taking a trip through South America.

Tener la palabra—to have the floor.

El señor Gómez tiene la palabra.
Mr. Gómez has the floor.

Tener presente (de) que—to bear in mind (that) . . .

Tenga presente (de) que necesito el dinero para pasado mañana, a más tardar.
Bear in mind that I need the money by the day after tomorrow, at the latest.

Tener prisa—to be in a hurry.

Cuando los vimos anoche, tenían mucha prisa.
When we saw them last night, they were in quite a hurry.

Tener que ver con—to have to do with.

No tenemos nada que ver con eso.
We have nothing to do with that.

Tener razón—to be right.

(1) Usted tiene razón.
You are right.

(2) Ellos no tienen razón.
They are wrong.

Un día sí y un día no (or **un día sí y otro no**)—Every other day.

Viene a verme un día sí y un día no.
He comes to see me every other day.

Valer la pena (de *plus infinitive*)—to be worth while; to be worth the trouble, or effort, to . . .

(1) No vale la pena.
It isn't worth the trouble.

(2) No vale la pena de pedirle nada.
It isn't worth the effort to ask him for anything.

¡Vaya!—Come now! You don't say! (*disbelief or jest*)

[33]

Venga lo que venga—Come what may.

Venga lo que venga, me quedaré aquí.
Come what may, I shall stay here.

Venirse abajo—to collapse; to fall.

Se ha venido abajo la nueva administración.
The new administration has collapsed.

Volver en sí—to recover one's senses, or consciousness; to come to.

A los cinco minutos volvió en sí.
He came to, five minutes later.

PART II

UNIVERSAL ADVANCED IDIOMS

PART II

UNIVERSAL ADVANCED IDIOMS

136 Idioms, etc., Common to All Spanish-Speaking People
Everywhere. This Second List is Indispensable to a Fluent
and Advanced Mastery of Spoken and Written Spanish. Here
is the Popular Everyday Language, Colloquialisms and Slang
of the Spanish-Speaking World.

A tontas y a locas—rashly; without thought; recklessly.

Esa muchacha lo hace todo a tontas y a locas.
That girl does everything recklessly.

A troche y moche—in confusion and hurry; pell-mell; helter-skelter.

El toro corría, embistiendo a troche y moche, por las calles.
The bull ran pell-mell through the streets, violently attacking
(all those in his path).

Agarrarlo con las manos en la masa—to catch one red-handed;
to catch one with the goods; to catch one in the act (of doing
something he shouldn't).

Lo agarré con las manos en la masa.
I caught him red-handed.

Agotarle la paciencia—to try one's patience.

Ese tipo me agota la paciencia.
That fellow tries my patience.

Andar de boca en boca—to be the talk of the town.

Su nombre anda de boca en boca.

He's the talk of the town.

Andar de la Ceca a la Meca—to go from pillar to post (without accomplishing anything).

He andado de la Ceca a la Meca buscando casa.

I've gone from pillar to post looking for a house (and I didn't accomplish a thing!)

Andar(se) con rodeos—to beat around the bush.

¡No (se) ande con rodeos! Dígame lo que quiero saber.

Don't beat around the bush! Tell me what I want to know.

Buscar(le) tres pies al gato—to look for trouble; to pick a fight.

No le busque tres pies al gato.

Don't look for trouble.

Caer como maná del cielo—to come like manna from heaven; to come when most needed.

Los cinco dólares me cayeron como maná del cielo.

The five dollars came to me like manna from heaven.

Caérsele a uno la baba—to be gaga over something or someone (*lit.* to be drooling at the mouth).

Se le cae la baba por ella.

He's gaga over her.

Cargar con el muerto—(1) to get the blame, or suffer the consequences, for something you haven't done.
(2) to be left holding the bag.

(1) Juan rompió la ventana, pero yo cargué con el muerto.

John broke the window, but *I* got the blame (and suffered the consequences).

(2) Cuando llegó el tiempo de pagar la cuenta, como de costumbre, él cargó con el muerto.

When the time came to pay the bill, as usual, *he* was left holding the bag.

Codearse con—to rub elbows with . . .

Ellos se codean con la gente más rica de la ciudad.

They rub elbows with the richest people in the city.

Comerse a uno con los ojos—to feast one's eyes on one; to look at one with desire in your eyes (usually a girl).

Se la comía con los ojos.

He feasted his eyes on her.

Conocer (una cosa) como la palma de la mano—to know something from A to Z; to be thoroughly acquainted with a thing or situation.

Él conoce este pueblo como la palma de su mano.

He knows this town from A to Z.

Consultarlo con la almohada—to sleep on it; to think it over.

Consúltelo con la almohada.

Sleep on it. (Think it over.)

Correr a rienda suelta—to run full speed; to run wild.

Los dos caballos corrían a rienda suelta.

The two horses were running wild.

Creerse una (or la) gran cosa—to think oneself quite the thing.

Se cree una (*or* la) gran cosa.

(The *la* form, also used in Spain, is preferred in Mexico and some of the Central-American republics.)

He thinks himself quite the thing.

[39]

Dar de alta—to discharge (as a patient).

A los quince días me dieron de alta (del hospital).
Two weeks later they discharged me (from the hospital).

Dar de baja—to muster out (of service); to discharge from the army.

Después de unos cinco años en el ejército, le dieron de baja.
After some five years in the army, they mustered him out.

Dar en el clavo—to hit the nail on the head. (*fig.*)

¡Dió en el clavo!
You hit the nail on the head!

Dar (or **meter**) **gato por liebre**—to put it over on one (in the sense of misrepresenting on value received).

El hombre que me vendió esta máquina me dió (*or* metió) gato por liebre.
The man who sold me this machine sure put one over on me.

Dar calabazas—to jilt; to give one the gate, or the air.

Su novia le dió calabazas.
His girl-friend jilted him.

(NOTE: In parts of Central America, such as El Salvador, Guatemala, Costa Rica, **dar calabazas** often has the meaning of *to make jealous*, pertaining to matters of love, between novios):

Le está dando calabazas.
She's making him jealous.

Dar la lata—to bore to death (with a lot of talk).

Todos los días viene a darme la lata.
He comes and bores me to death every day.

Darle con la puerta en las narices—to shut the door in one's face.

Me dió con la puerta en las narices.
He shut the door in my face.

Darle un sablazo—to put the bite, or the pressure, on one for some money; to make a touch.

Vino a darme un sablazo.
He came to make a touch.

Darse bombo—to give oneself an air of importance (by making a lot of noise, or by talking about oneself).

Juanito se da mucho bombo.
Johnny gives himself quite an air of importance.

Darse ínfulas—to put on airs.

Tu amigo se da muchas ínfulas.
Your friend sure puts on airs.

Darse tono—to put on airs.

Aquella muchacha se da mucho tono.
That girl puts on a lot of airs.

Decirle cuatro verdades—to tell one off; to give one a piece of your mind.

Le dije cuatro verdades.
I gave him a piece of my mind.

Decírselo en su (propia) cara—to tell one right to his face.

Me lo dijo en mi (propia) cara.
He told me right to my face.

Dejarlo plantado—to stand one up (on a date or appointment).

Tenía un compromiso con mi novia y me dejó plantado.
I had a date with my girl-friend and she stood me up.

[41]

Devanarse los sesos—to wrack one's brains.

Me estoy devanando los sesos para solucionar este problema.
I'm wracking my brains to solve this problem.

Dormir a pierna suelta—to sleep like a log; to sleep soundly.

Anoche dormí a pierna suelta.
Last night I slept like a log.

Dormir la mona—to sleep it off. (*ref. to a drunken condition*)

Está durmiendo la mona.
He's sleeping it off.

Dormirse sobre (or en) sus laureles—to rest on one's laurels.

Él nunca se duerme sobre sus laureles.
He never rests on his laurels.

Echar en saco roto—to disregard entirely (what one says).

Le dí unos buenos consejos, pero los echó en saco roto.
I gave him some good advice, but he disregarded it entirely.

Echar flores (or piropos)—to flatter, or compliment (mostly a
girl or woman).

No me eche flores.
Don't flatter me.

Echar la casa por la ventana—to blow the works; to spend more
than one has.

Fuimos anoche a una fiesta, y la dueña echó la casa por la
ventana.
We went to a party last night, and the hostess really blew the
works.

Echar una cana al aire—to go out for a good time; to go out on a fling; to go out on a lark.

Vamos a echar una cana al aire.
Let's go out for a good time.

Empinar el codo—to hit the bottle.

Siempre está empinando el codo.
He's always hitting the bottle.

Encogerse de hombros—to shrug one's shoulders.

Cuando le preguntamos si quería ir al cine, se encogió de hombros.
When we asked him if he wanted to go to the movies, he shrugged his shoulders.

Encontrar (encontrarse con, or hallar) la horma de su zapato —to meet one's match, or waterloo; to get it in the neck.

Algún día te vas a encontrar con la horma de tu zapato.
Some day you're going to meet your waterloo.

Entrar (or andar) como Pedro por su casa.
(1) to be perfectly at home in a place; to know one's way around. (2) to *make oneself* perfectly at home (*may* indicate abusing privileges).

(1) Aquí ando como Pedro por su casa.
I know my way around here.

(2) Entró como Pedro por su casa.
He made himself perfectly at home.

Escarmentar en cabeza ajena—to profit by the mistakes of others.

Hay que escarmentar en cabeza ajena.
One should profit by the mistakes of others.

[43]

Estar con un pie en la sepultura—to have one foot in the grave. (*fig.*)

Cuando lo conocí por primera vez, estaba con un pie en la sepultura.
When I first met him, he had one foot in the grave.

Estar en ayunas—to be in the dark (about something); to be unaware, or uninformed.

Estoy completamente en ayunas.
I'm completely in the dark about it.

Estar en la luna—to be absorbed in other thoughts; to be heedless, or inattentive; to have one's mind elsewhere.

Le expliqué cómo hacerlo, pero él estaba en la luna.
I explained to him how to do it, but he was absorbed in other thoughts.

Estar en las últimas—to be on one's last legs.

Creo que nuestro amigo está en las últimas.
I think our friend is on his last legs.

Estar entre la espada y la pared—to be between the devil and the deep blue sea.

Estoy entre la espada y la pared. ¿Qué voy a hacer?
I'm between the devil and the deep blue sea. What am I going to do?

Estar hasta la coronilla—to be fed up; to have stood as much as possible.

Tú me agotas la paciencia. ¡Estoy hasta la coronilla!
You try my patience. I'm fed up! (I've stood as much as possible!)

Estar hecho una sopa—to be drenched through and through; to be soaking wet.

Pobre muchacha, estás hecha una sopa.
Poor girl, you're drenched through and through.

Estirar la pata—to kick the bucket; to kick off; to die.

Al día siguiente estiró la pata.
He kicked off the next day.

Hablar hasta por los codos—to talk a blue streak.

Mi suegra habla hasta por los codos.
My mother-in-law talks a blue streak.

Hacer castillos en el aire—to build air-castles, or castles in the air.

Pasa la mayor parte del tiempo haciendo castillos en el aire.
He spends most of the time building air-castles.

Hacer (una) de las suyas—to play, or be up to, one's usual tricks; to run true to type.

Está haciendo (una) de las suyas.
He's up to his usual tricks.

Hacer de tripas corazón—to pluck up courage; to pull oneself together.

Después de esa desgracia, hice de tripas corazón y seguí adelante.
After that misfortune, I pulled myself together and carried on.

Hacer las paces—to make up; to bury the hatchet. (*fig.*)

Bésame, querida, y hagamos las paces.
Kiss me, sweetheart, and let's make up.

[45]

Hacer pucheros—to snivel (as a child, before crying).

María, ¡no hagas pucheros!
Mary, don't start sniveling!

Hacer su agosto—(1) to take advantage for one's own profit; to make hay while the sun shines; to make one's harvest. (2) to go to town on something.

(1) Está haciendo su agosto.
He's making hay while the sun shines.

(2) Hizo su agosto en el "bufet."
He really went to town on the buffet supper.

Hacerle gracia—to strike one funny.

Su informe me hizo gracia.
Your report struck me funny.

Hacerle una mala pasada—to play a dirty, or mean, trick on one.

Me hizo una mala pasada.
He played a dirty trick on me.

Hacerse de la vista gorda—to pretend not to see what's going on; to look the other way.

El policía la vió robar una manzana, pero se hizo de la vista gorda.
The policeman saw her steal an apple, but he looked the other way.

Hacerse de rogar—to like to be coaxed; to play hard to get.

Todas las muchachas que yo conozco se hacen de rogar.
All the girls I know play hard to get.

Hacerse el sordo—to turn a deaf ear.

Le pedimos que nos ayudara, pero se hizo el sordo.
We asked him to help us, but he turned a deaf ear.

[46]

Hacérsele agua la boca—to have one's mouth watering (in anticipation).

Se le hace agua la boca.
His mouth is watering.

Hacérsele un nudo en la garganta—to get a lump in one's throat; to be speechless (on account of emotion).

Se me hizo un nudo en la garganta.
I got a lump in my throat.

Ir al grano—to get down to brass tacks; to get down to cases.

¡Vamos al grano!
Let's get down to brass tacks.

Ir de juerga—to go out on a spree; to go out and have a good time.

Anoche fuimos de juerga.
Last night we went out on a spree.

Ir de parranda (also **parrandear**)—to go out on a spree; to go out and make merry.

Esta noche vamos de parranda (*or* vamos a parrandear).
Tonight we're going out and make merry.

Ir por lana y salir trasquilado—to get the tables turned on one (in the sense of to come out on the short side). (*Used most always in past tense*)

Juan fué donde su amigo a pedirle un dólar, y aquél no sólo no le dió nada, sino que le pidió prestados cincuenta centavos.
John went to see his friend to ask him for a dollar, and not only didn't his friend give him anything, but borrowed fifty cents, to boot.

(En otras palabras, **Fué por lana y salió trasquilado**).
(In other words, John got the tables turned on him).

Irse para el otro mundo (or **barrio**)—to die; to pass away; to pass on to the Great Beyond.

Se fué para el otro mundo.
He passed away.

Írsele la lengua—to have a slip of the tongue; to let something out unintentionally; to let the cat out of the bag.

¡Caramba! Se me fué la lengua!
Darn it, I let the cat out of the bag!

Jugarle una mala partida (or **pasada**)—to play a dirty, or mean, trick on one.

Me jugaron una mala partida (*or* pasada).
They played a dirty trick on me.

Lavarse las manos (como Pilatos)—to wash one's hands of the whole affair.

Me lavo las manos.
I wash my hands of the whole affair.

Llamar (or **decir**) **al pan pan, y al vino vino**—to call a spade a spade.

Es un hombre que (le) llama al pan pan, y al vino vino.
He's a man who calls a spade a spade.

Llevar la batuta—to be the leader; to wear the pants.

Mi esposa es quien lleva la batuta en nuestra casa.
My wife is the one who wears the pants in our household.

Llevarse la palma—to carry away the honors; to rank first.

En química, Juan siempre se lleva la palma.
In chemistry, John always carries away the honors.

Llorar a moco tendido—to cry like a baby. (*fig.*)

El hombre lloraba a moco tendido.
The man cried like a baby.

Llover a cántaros—to pour; to rain pitchforks; to rain cats and
  dogs.

¡Está lloviendo a cántaros!
It's raining cats and dogs!

Meter la pata—to put one's foot in it. (*fig.*); to make a faux pas.

¡Tonto, siempre metes la pata!
Idiot! You're always putting your foot in it!

Meter la nariz (or **las narices**) **en todas partes**—to be a busy-
  body; to stick one's nose into other people's affairs.

¡Estás metiendo la nariz en todas partes!
You're a busy-body!

Meter su (or **la**) **cuchara**—to butt in; to stick one's two cents in.

Estábamos hablando, y Carlitos metió su (*or* la) cuchara.
We were speaking and Charlie butted in.

Meterse a redentor—to stick one's neck out (only to get it
  chopped off). (*fig.*)

No te metas a redentor.
Don't stick your neck out!

Meterse en camisa de once varas—to get oneself in a nice fix
  (undertaking something one should not attempt, because it
  is too big or not within one's power or means, or is none of
  one's business. Hence, almost the equivalent of *to bite off
  more than one can chew,* if any of the above meanings fit the
  individual case).

Respaldar esa compañía es una cosa muy peligrosa. ¡No te metas en camisa de once varas!
Backing that company is a very risky thing. Don't bite off more than you can chew!

Meterse en honduras—to get into trouble; to get into deep waters.

No lo hagas, que te vas a meter en honduras.
Don't do it, because you'll get into trouble.

Meterse en un lío—to get oneself in a jam.

Se metió en un lío.
He got himself in a jam.

Mirar de reojo—to look (at one) out of the corner of one's eye.

Su jefe lo estaba mirando de reojo.
His boss was looking at him out of the corner of his eye.

No atreverse a decir (ni) esta boca es mía—not to be able to call one's soul one's own; not to dare open one's mouth. (*fig.*)

Desde que se casó, no se atreve a decir (ni) esta boca es mía.
He's not able to call his soul his own since he got married.

No dar su (or el) brazo a torcer—to be stubborn and not to give in.

Su señora no da su brazo a torcer.
His wife is stubborn and won't give in.

No dar pie con bola—to make a mess of things; not to do things right.

Ni el uno ni el otro da pie con bola.
Neither one of them does things right.

[50]

No poder ver a uno ni pintado } —not to be able to bear one; ni en pintura } not to be able to stand the sight of one.

La odia tanto que no la puede ver ni pintada (*or* ni en pintura).
He hates her so much that he can't stand the sight of her.

No saber en lo que se mete—not to know what one is letting oneself in for; not to know what one is getting into.

Ellos no sabían en lo que se iban a meter.
They didn't know what they were letting themselves in for.

No tragar a uno (or **no poder tragarlo**)—not to be able to stand one; not to be able to stomach one.

Son tan antipáticos que no los trago (*or* no los puedo tragar).
They are so disagreeable that I can't stomach them.

No tener (ni) donde (or **en que**, or **sobre que**) **caer(se) muerto**—not to have a penny to one's name.

Es tan pobre que no tiene (ni) donde caer(se) muerto.
—or—
Es tan pobre que no tiene en (*or* sobre) que caer muerto.
He hasn't a penny to his name.

No tener pelos en la lengua—to speak one's mind freely; to be outspoken.

Margarita no tiene pelos en la lengua.
Margaret speaks her mind freely.

Pagar el pato—(1) to get the blame, or suffer the consequences, for something you haven't done. (2) to be left holding the bag.

Yo pagué el pato.
I got the blame (and suffered the consequences).
—or—
I was left holding the bag.
    (NOTE: For a more complete idea as to how this idiom may be used in a given situation, see **cargar con el muerto**)

[51]

Pagar los platos rotos—*Same as above.*

El pagó los platos rotos.
He got the blame (and suffered the consequences).
—or—
He was left holding the bag.

Pasar las de Caín—to have a hard, or tough, time of it. (*mostly finan.*)

Estoy pasando las de Caín.
I'm having a tough time of it.

Pedir(le) peras al olmo—to expect, ask, or look, for the impossible.

Pedirle dinero a ese hombre es como pedirle peras al olmo.
To get any money from that man is asking the impossible.

Perder la chaveta—to lose one's mind; to become crazy.

Cuando le dijeron que se le había muerto su esposa, perdió la chaveta.
When they told him that his wife had died, he lost his mind.

Perder los estribos—to lose one's balance. (*fig.*) ; to lose control of oneself; to go to pieces.

No hay que perder los estribos.
Don't lose your balance.

Poner el dedo en la llaga—to touch a (or one's) sore spot.

Yo hablaba de la embriaguez en presencia de Juan, que es un borracho confirmado.
I was speaking about drunkenness in the presence of John, who is a confirmed drunkard.

(Así, puse el dedo en la llaga).
(Thus, I hit his sore spot).

[52]

Poner el grito en el cielo—to raise Cain (in the sense of complaining loudly—usually without justification).

Cuando me vió bailando con su hija, puso el grito en el cielo.
When he saw me dancing with his daughter, he raised Cain.

Poner los puntos sobre las íes—to make, or get, things clear; to clarify the situation.

Vamos a poner los puntos sobre las íes.
Let's get things clear.

Poner por las nubes—to speak very highly of; to praise to the skies.

Tu profesor te puso por las nubes.
Your teacher praised you to the skies.

Ponerlo a raya—to put one in his place; to hold one in check.

Lo puse a raya.
I put him in his place.

Ponerlo en ridículo—to make a fool out of one; to make one look ridiculous.

Trató de ponerme en ridículo.
He tried to make me look ridiculous.

Quedarse con un (or el) pie en el estribo—to be all set to go (implying disappointment at the last minute).

Me quedé con un pie en el estribo.
I was all set to go (and disappointed at the last minute).

Quedarse para vestir santos—to be a spinster, or old maid.

(NOTE: This idiom is used almost always in the PAST TENSE —with PRESENT significance.)

Se quedó para vestir santos.
She's an old maid. (She never married.)

Quemarse las pestañas—to burn the midnight oil; to study very diligently.

Lincoln fué un hombre que se quemaba las pestañas. Finalmente llegó a ser presidente de los Estados Unidos.

Lincoln was a man who would burn the midnight oil. Finally, he became President of the United States.

Reír a mandíbula batiente—to rock with laughter; to laugh heartily.

Le contamos un chiste, y rió a mandíbula batiente.

We told him a joke and he rocked with laughter.

Saber al dedillo—to know to a T; to know perfectly.

Lo sé al dedillo.

I know it to a T.

Saber uno donde le aprieta el zapato—to know one's onions.

El sabe donde le aprieta el zapato.

He knows his onions.

> (NOTE: One of our English-Spanish dictionaries renders this idiom by its literal meaning, e.g., *to know where the shoe pinches,* but we do not believe the above covers *our* interpretation of this phrase.)

Sacar la cara por uno—to go to bat for one; to go to the front for one; to take one's part.

Saqué la cara por tí, pero tú no lo aprecias.

I went to bat for you, but you don't appreciate it.

Sacar las uñas—to show one's true colors.

Ya sacó las uñas.

Now he has shown his true colors.

[54]

Sacarlo de quicio—to try one's patience; to exasperate one beyond words.

Ese tipo me saca de quicio.
That guy exasperates me beyond words.

Sacarlo de sus casillas—to drive one crazy. (*fig.*)

Mi hermana menor me saca de mis casillas.
My younger sister drives me crazy.

Salir con el rabo entre las piernas—to go away feeling very humiliated; to go away with one's tail between one's legs.

Salió con el rabo entre las piernas.
He went away with his tail between his legs.

Salirle el tiro por la culata—to have something back-fire on one.

Juan trató de indisponerme con mi jefe, pero éste lo despidió por chismoso.
John tried to put me in bad with my boss, but the boss fired him for being a tattle-tale.

(En otras palabras, le salió el tiro por la culata.)
(In other words, it back-fired on him!)

Salirse con la suya—to have, or get, one's own way.

Por fin, se salió con la suya.
She finally got her own way.

Salirse por la tangente—to avoid, or sidestep, the issue.

No te salgas por la tangente.
Don't avoid the issue.

Sondear el ambiente—to get the lay of the land; to see what's what.

Vamos a sondear el ambiente.
Let's get the lay of the land.

[55]

Sudar la gota gorda—to sweat profusely; to be dripping with perspiration (from humiliation, work or heat).

(1) El profesor le regañó en presencia de toda la clase y créame, ¡sudó la gota gorda!

The teacher bawled him out in front of the whole class and, believe me, he was really sweating!

(2) Lo ví componiendo su automóvil, y estaba sudando la gota gorda.

I saw him fixing his automobile, and he was sweating profusely.

(3) ¡Qué día más caluroso! Todo el mundo está sudando la gota gorda.

What a hot day! Everybody is dripping with perspiration.

Tener que vérselas con uno—(1) to have a bone to pick with one.
(2) to have to answer to one (in the sense of having to contend with, or account to, one).

(1) Tengo que vérmelas con usted.
I have a bone to pick with you.

(2) Salió sin permiso, y cuando regresó se las tuvo que ver con su mamá.

He went out without permission, and when he returned he had to answer to his mother.

Tenerlo entre ojos—to have taken a dislike to one; to have a grudge against one.

El jefe me tiene entre ojos.
The boss has taken a dislike to me.

Tocarle en lo vivo—to hurt one to the quick.

Eso me tocó en lo vivo.
That hurt me to the quick.

Tomar a pecho—to take to heart.

No lo tome a pecho.
Don't take it to heart.

Tomar el rábano por las hojas—to misinterpret something; to take something the wrong way; to jump to the wrong conclusion.

Tomaste el rábano por las hojas.
You took it the wrong way.

Tomar las de Villadiego—to take to one's heels; to beat it.

Tomó las de Villadiego.
He took to his heels. (He beat it.)

Tomar por su cuenta—to attend to personally.

Lo tomo por mi cuenta.
I'll attend to it personally.

Tomarle el pelo—to kid one.

Le está tomando el pelo.
He's kidding you.

Venir al pelo—to fit the case to a T.

Eso viene al pelo.
That fits the case to a T.

Venir (como) a pedir de boca—to come as if in answer to one's prayers.

Vino (como) a pedir de boca.
It came as if in answer to our prayers.

[57]

Ver la paja en el ojo ajeno—to see other people's faults, but fail to see one's own.

> (NOTE: The *el* of the first part is generally omitted in Spanish America.)

Ese tipo ve la paja en el ojo ajeno (y no la viga en el suyo).
That fellow sees other people's faults, but fails to see his own.

Vivir de gorra—to sponge; to be a sponger; to be a parasite.

> (NOTE: Not popular in Argentina, Paraguay, Uruguay and Chile.)

¡Tú vives de gorra! Nunca pagas nada.
You're a sponger! You never pay for anything.

TABLE OF CONVERSIONS

PART II

Idiom	Converted to	In (Country)
A tontas y a locas	a tontas y a ciegas	COSTA RICA
Agarrarlo con las manos en la masa	agarrarlo con la masa en la mano	NICARAGUA
Buscar(le) tres pies al gato	buscarle las cinco patas al gato	CHILE
Caérsele a uno la baba	salírsele a uno la baba	PANAMA
Dar calabazas	dar *de* calabazas **or better** darle el pasaporte	NICARAGUA
Darle un sablazo	pegarle un sablazo	BOLIVIA
Decirle cuatro verdades	decirle cuatro	COSTA RICA
Dormir la mona	dormir la juma	EL SALVADOR, PANAMA, COLOMBIA, VENEZUELA, (COSTA RICA)
Echar la casa por la ventana	tirar la casa por la ventana	PERU, CUBA and PARAGUAY
Escarmentar en cabeza ajena	escarmentar en cuero ajeno	BOLIVIA
Estar entre la espada y la pared	estar entre la cruz y la espada	BOLIVIA
Estar hasta la coronilla	estar hasta el copete	(NICARAGUA)
Estirar la pata	estirar los hules	EL SALVADOR (and is also used in Guatemala)
Hacer de tripas corazón	hacer de tripas corazones	NICARAGUA
Hacerse de la vista gorda	hacer la vista gorda	ARGENTINA, CHILE, URUGUAY, PARAGUAY and PERU

[59]

TABLE OF CONVERSIONS

PART II (Continued)

Idiom	Converted to	In (Country)
Hacerse de rogar	hacerse del rogar	MEXICO
	hacerse rogar	HONDURAS, NICARAGUA, COSTA RICA, VENEZUELA and ARGENTINA
Meter su (or la) cuchara	meter su (or la) cucharada	COLOMBIA
No dar pie con bola	no dar pie en bola	CHILE and PARAGUAY
	no dar bola	COLOMBIA
Poner el grito en el cielo	poner el grito al cielo	BOLIVIA and NICARAGUA
	pegar el grito al cielo	NICARAGUA, COSTA RICA and PANAMA
Poner los puntos sobre las íes	poner el punto sobre las íes	ARGENTINA and PARAGUAY
Quedarse para vestir santos	quedarse vistiendo santos	NICARAGUA
Saber al dedillo	saber al caletre	VENEZUELA
Sacar la cara por uno	poner la cara por uno	COLOMBIA and VENEZUELA
Sacar las uñas	mostrar las uñas	BOLIVIA
Salir con el rabo entre las piernas	salir con la cola entre las patas	GUATEMALA, EL SALVADOR and (HONDURAS)
Salirse por la tangente	irse por la tangente	CUBA
Sondear el ambiente	tantear el ambiente	ARGENTINA, PERU, CHILE and (BOLIVIA)

[60]

PART III

FAMILIAR EXPRESSIONS: HUMOROUS, SLANG AND IDIOMATIC EXPRESSIONS IN DAILY USE THROUGHOUT THE SPANISH-SPEAKING WORLD

PART III

FAMILIAR EXPRESSIONS: HUMOROUS, SLANG AND IDIOMATIC EXPRESSIONS IN DAILY USE THROUGHOUT THE SPANISH-SPEAKING WORLD

A las mil maravillas—wonderfully well; like a million dollars.

Juan: —¿Cómo se siente?
Felipe: —¡A las mil maravillas!

John: How do you feel?
Philip: Like a million dollars!

¡A otro perro con ese hueso!—Tell it to the marines! Tell it to Sweeney!

¡Aquí hay gato encerrado!—There's something strange going on around here! There's something fishy going on around here!

Aquí pasándola—Just getting along. Just making ends meet. So-so.

Carlos: —¿Cómo le va?
Pablo: —Aquí pasándola.

Charles: How goes it with you?
Paul: Just getting along.

¡Así es la vida!—Such is life!

[63]

Contigo, pan y cebolla—(An equivalent in English would be something along the lines of *I'd be happy on bread and onions, so long as I have you.* —or— *I'll be poor, but at least I'll have you.*)

Cuando San Juan baje el dedo—(This expression, alluding to the statue of Saint John, the Baptist, indicates that which is not likely to happen. An equivalent in English would be something along the lines of *When hell freezes over.*)

> (NOTE: It is not popular in Argentina, Chile, Bolivia, Paraguay and Uruguay. *Agache* is preferred to **baje** in Colombia and Venezuela; also parts of Panama and Ecuador.)

En los quintos infiernos —or— **En el quinto infierno**—Way out to Hell-'n'-gone.

(1) Used as a complete thought, as in the above phrase.

(2) Vive en los quintos infiernos. —or— Vive en el quinto infierno.
He lives way out to Hell-'n'-gone.

En menos que (or de lo que) canta un gallo—In two shakes of a lamb's tail. —or— Before you can say Jack Robinson.

En todas partes cuecen habas—That can happen anywhere. —or— It happens in the best of families.

> (NOTE: In Spanish America, **cuecen** is generally preceded by **se**, e.g., *En todas partes se cuecen habas.*)

(En) total, nada—In short, nothing happened. —or— Nothing came of it.

(1) Used as a complete thought, as in the above phrase.

(2) Le he enviado flores, le he escrito cartas—y en total, nada.
I've sent her flowers, I've written her letters—and nothing came of it.

[64]

En un abrir y cerrar de ojos—In a split second. In the twinkling of an eye.

Es como hablarle a una pared (or **piedra**)—It's like talking to the four walls.

(1) Used as a complete thought, as in the above phrase.

(2) Hablarle a ella es como hablarle a una pared.
Speaking to her is like talking to the four walls.

Eso es harina de otro costal—That's a horse of another color.

¡Eso nada más me faltaba!—That's all I need(ed)! (*exasperation*)

Feo como él solo }
Fea como ella sola }—As ugly as can be. As ugly as sin.

¡Hay moros en la costa!—Jiggers! The coast is not clear!

¡La cosa está que arde!—Things are getting pretty hot! (indicating that the situation is tense).

La verdad clara y desnuda (or **clara y pelada**)—The truth, pure and simple. The pure, unadulterated truth.

Lo que te he dicho es la verdad clara y desnuda.
What I have told you is the pure, unadulterated truth.

(NOTE: The *clara y pelada* alternative is preferred in certain parts of Spanish America.)

Lo mismo da—It all adds up to the same thing.

Lo que pasó, pasó—What's past is past. —or— Let bygones be bygones.

Más viejo que Matusalén—As old as Methuselah. —or— As old as the hills.

Ni chicha ni limonada—Neither fish nor fowl (nor good red herring).

(1) Used as a short phrase, as above.

(2) Dolores: —¿Qué le parece el arte futurista?
Antonio: —Me parece que no es ni chicha ni limonada.

Dolores: What do you think of futuristic art?
Anthony: To me, it's neither fish nor fowl.

¡Ni en sueños!—I wouldn't dream of (doing) it!

No cante victoria—Don't brag about it. Don't be too sure. (an indication in the speaker's mind that something might yet happen to spoil it.)

Juan: —Estamos ganando la guerra.
Felipe: —No cante victoria (todavía).

John: We're winning the war.
Philip: Don't be too sure.

¡No faltaba más!—That caps (*or* capped) the climax! That's the last straw! The straw that broke the camel's back!

No le hace—It makes no difference.

¡No quisiera estar en su pellejo!—I wouldn't want to be in your (his, her, or their) shoes!

No viene al caso—That's not the point.

¿Qué hubo?—What's up? —or— What's cooking?

(NOTE: This expression is usually pronounced very rapidly—as if it were written as one word.)

¿Qué mosca te ha picado?—What's eating you?

(NOTE: In Mexico, *¿Qué te pica?*)

[66]

¿Qué tal?—How goes it? Hi'ya? Whaddaya say?

¿Quién le pone el cascabel al gato?—Who's going to tackle the problem?

Los empleados de nuestra oficina quieren un aumento de sueldo, y para conseguir sus demandas uno de ellos tendrá que hablar al jefe.

The employees in our office want a raise in salary and, in order for them to get their demands, one of them will have to speak to the boss.

¿Quién le pone el cascabel al gato?

Who's going to tackle the boss?

Se armó la (or una) de San Quintín—All Hell broke loose.

(1) Used as a complete thought, as above.

(2) Su novia lo encontró con otra muchacha, y se armó la de San Quintín.

His fiancée found him with another girl, and all Hell broke loose.

¡Se me acabó la paciencia!—My patience is at an end!

¡Son cosas de la vida!—Such is life!

Todo el santo día—All the livelong day. All the blessed day.

La niña lloraba todo el santo día.

The child cried all the livelong day:

¡Trato hecho!—It's a deal.

Guillermo: —Le pagaré quinientos dólares por su automóvil.

Jorge: —¡Trato hecho!

William: I'll pay you $500 for your car.
George: It's a deal!

[67]

¡Váyase con la música a otra parte!—Go peddle your fish some place else!

Viento en popa—Splendid(ly)! Couldn't be better!

Pedro: —¿Cómo andan los negocios?
Juan: —¡Viento en popa!

Peter: How's business?
John: Couldn't be better!

Vivito y coleando—Going strong. —or— Alive and kicking.

Pensaban que se iba a morir, pero todavía está vivito y coleando.
They thought he was going to die, but he's still alive and kicking.

¡Ya lo creo!—Yes, indeed! —or— I should say so!

PART IV

AXIOMS, PROVERBS, ADAGES, APHORISMS AND MAXIMS, IN POPULAR USE THROUGHOUT THE SPANISH-SPEAKING WORLD

PART IV

AXIOMS, PROVERBS, ADAGES, APHORISMS AND MAXIMS, IN POPULAR USE THROUGHOUT THE SPANISH-SPEAKING WORLD

A caballo regalado no se le mira el diente (or el colmillo)
Never look a gift horse in the mouth.

A donde (or al país que) fueres, haz lo que vieres
When in Rome, do as the Romans do.

A espaldas vueltas, memorias muertas
Out of sight, out of mind.

> (NOTE: The above maxim is very academic, and is found mostly in literary works.)

A quien le venga el guante, que se lo plante
If the shoe fits, wear it.

Agua que no has de beber, déjala correr
If it's not for you, let it alone. —or— What's not for you to enjoy, let the other fellow have.

Al buen entendedor, pocas palabras
A word to the wise is sufficient.

Al que le pique, que se rasque
If the shoe fits, wear it.

[71]

Aunque la mona se vista de seda, mona se queda—(usually applied to an ugly woman or girl, indicating that, no matter how much adorning or dressing up she may do, she alters only her *superficial* appearance. The Velázquez Spanish-English dictionary offers: *Dress a monkey as you will, it remains a monkey still.*)

Ayúdate que Dios te ayudará
God helps those who help themselves.

Cada loco con su tema
Everyone to his hobby.

Cada oveja con su pareja
Birds of a feather flock together. —or— Like seeks like. (*sarc.*)

Con la vara que midas, serás medido
As ye judge others, so shall ye be judged.

Cuando el río suena, agua (or piedras) lleva
Where there's smoke, there's fire.

> (NOTE: *Trae,* as an alternative for **lleva,** is frequently used in certain Spanish-American countries.)

(De) donde menos se espera (or se piensa), salta la liebre
You don't know what to expect. —or— Things happen when you least expect them to.

De tal palo, tal astilla
A chip off the old block. —or— Like father, like son.

Del árbol caído todos hacen leña—(figurative proverbial expression to the effect that when a person is down, people will kick him.)

Del dicho al hecho hay mucho (or un gran) trecho
To say a thing and to do a thing are two different stories. —or— It's easier said than done.

Dime con quien andas, y te diré quien eres
Tell me who your company is, and I'll tell you who you are. —or— A man is known by the company he keeps.

[72]

Dios los cría y ellos se juntan
Birds of a feather flock together. (*sarc.*)

Donde hubo fuego, hay cenizas—(This proverbial expression, used in matters pertaining to love, indicates that a person is still *carrying a torch* for the other person involved.)

El buey solo, bien se lame—(Proverbial expression indicating one's preference to be by oneself than have to put up with bad company.)

El camarón que se duerme, se lo lleva la corriente—(Proverbial expression to the effect that the fellow who isn't on his toes will get lost in the shuffle.)

El hábito no hace al monje
Clothes don't make the man.

El hombre propone y Dios dispone
Man proposes and God disposes.

El que a hierro (or a cuchillo) mata, a hierro (or a cuchillo) muere
He who lives by the sword, dies by the sword.

El que (or quien) busca, encuentra
Seek and ye shall find.

El que espera, desespera
He who lives in hope, dies in despair.

El que la hace, la paga
As ye sow, so shall ye reap.

El que mucho habla, mucho yerra
He who talks a lot, makes many mistakes.

El que quiera (azul) celeste, que le cueste

If you want something badly enough, you must pay for it. —or— If you want something badly enough, you must be prepared to work for it.

> (NOTE: The addition of *azul* is preferred in Spain and Cuba.)

El que se mete a redentor, sale (or muere) crucificado—(Self-explanatory proverbial expression to the effect that one shouldn't "stick his neck out.")

En boca cerrada no entra(n) mosca(s)

Silence is golden. —or— It pays to hold one's tongue.

La cabra (siempre) tira al monte

What's bred in the bone will come out in the flesh.

La experiencia cría ciencia. —or— **La experiencia hace al maestro**

Practice makes perfect.

La letra con sangre entra

Learning comes the hard way. —or— Learning comes with blood. —or— Those who would succeed must work with a will.

La ropa sucia se lava en la casa

Don't wash your dirty linen in public. —or— Keep the family skeletons in the closet.

Más vale pájaro en mano que ciento volando

A bird in the hand is worth two in the bush.

Más vale tarde que nunca

Better late than never.

Más vale solo que mal acompañado

It's better to be alone than have to put up with bad company.

No es oro todo lo que reluce (or brilla)

All that glitters is not gold.

No es tan fiero el león como lo pintan
His bark is worse than his bite.

No hay mal que por bien no venga
It's an ill wind that blows nobody good.

No hay peor sordo que el que no quiere oír
No one is so deaf as he who will not hear.

No hay rosa sin espinas
Every rose has its thorn.

No por mucho madrugar, amanece más temprano
No matter how early you get up, you cannot hasten the dawn
(meaning, of course, that you cannot rush the natural course
of things).

No se ganó Zamora en una hora
Rome wasn't built in a day.

> (NOTE: The above proverb is very academic, and is found
> mostly in literary works.)

Ojos que no ven, corazón que no siente
What we don't see, doesn't hurt us (in the sense that we are not
affected emotionally by people or situations when we are not
present).

Perro que ladra no muerde
A barking dog never bites.

Poco a poco se va (or se anda) lejos
Little by little, one goes a long way.

(Que) con su pan se lo coma
That's his own affair. (*contempt or indifference only*)

Quien (or el que) a solas se ríe, de sus maldades se acuerda—
> (This expression, or maxim, is applicable when, in a group
> of people, something is said which causes one particular
> person to smile or laugh. The meaning conveyed, and the
> innuendo directed toward that person, is: "He who laughs
> alone is remembering some wicked instances in his OWN
> life.")

Querer es poder

Where there's a will, there's a way.

Quien mucho abarca, poco aprieta

Grasp all, lose all. —or— Grasp no more than your hand will
 hold.

Un clavo saca otro clavo

One nail drives out another. —or— One grief cures another.
 —or— One excess cures another.

TABLE OF CONVERSIONS

PART IV

Axiom, Proverb, Adage, etc.	Converted to	In (Country)
A caballo regalado no se le mira el diente (or el colmillo)	A caballo regalado no se le busca (el) colmillo.	NICARAGUA, COSTA RICA and PANAMA
	A caballo dado no se le ve (el) colmillo.	MEXICO
	A macho regalado no se le busca colmillo.	HONDURAS and EL SALVADOR
A donde (or al país que) fueres, haz lo que vieres	En el país en que estuvieres, haz lo que vieres.	BOLIVIA
	A la tierra que fueres, haz lo que vieres.	HONDURAS and VENEZUELA
	Al que le caiga el guante, que se lo plante.	COLOMBIA, HONDURAS and NICARAGUA
A quien le venga el guante, que se lo plante	Al que le venga el guante, que se lo chante.	PERU
	Al que le toque el guante, que se lo chante.	BOLIVIA
	Al que le toque el guante, que se lo plante.	EL SALVADOR
	Al que le caiga la chupa, que se la ponga.	VENEZUELA
	Al que le venga el sayo, que se lo ponga.	CHILE
	Al que (or a quien) le venga el saco, que se lo ponga.	MEXICO
Al buen entendedor, pocas palabras	Al entendido—por señas.	HONDURAS and NICARAGUA
	Al buen entendedor, con dos palabras basta.	CUBA
De tal palo, tal astilla	De tal tronco, tal rama.	GUATEMALA
	De tal tronco, tal astilla.	BOLIVIA

[77]

TABLE OF CONVERSIONS

PART IV (Continued)

Axiom, Proverb, Adage, etc.	Converted to	In (Country)
Dios los cría y ellos se juntan	Dios los cría y el diablo los junta.	NICARAGUA, COSTA RICA, EL SALVADOR and GUATEMALA
Donde hubo fuego, hay cenizas	Donde hubo fuego, cenizas quedan.	CHILE and BOLIVIA
	Donde camotes se asaron, cenizas quedan.	PERU
	Donde hubo fuego, rescoldo queda.	MEXICO
La letra con sangre entra	La letra entra con sangre.	BOLIVIA
La ropa sucia se lava en la casa	Los trapos sucios se lavan en la casa.	COSTA RICA
Más vale pájaro en mano que ciento volando	Más vale pájaro en mano que cien volando.	CUBA, PANAMA, COSTA RICA, NICARAGUA, HONDURAS and ARGENTINA
	Más vale pájaro en mano que chivato en pampa.	PERU
No es tan fiero el león como lo pintan	No es tan bravo el león como lo pintan.	MEXICO
Ojos que no ven, corazón que no siente	Ojos que no ven, corazón no siente.	BOLIVIA
Quien (or el que) a solas se ríe, de sus maldades se acuerda	Replace **maldades** with *picardías*	ARGENTINA, PARAGUAY, COLOMBIA; also ECUADOR, which prefers *solo* to **a solas.**

PART V

IDIOMS, EXPRESSIONS, ETC., PECULIAR TO INDIVIDUAL SPANISH-AMERICAN REPUBLICS

PART V

IDIOMS, EXPRESSIONS, ETC., PECULIAR TO INDIVIDUAL SPANISH-AMERICAN REPUBLICS: INCLUDING SOME OF THEIR MOST POPULAR COLLOQUIALISMS AND SLANG

ARGENTINA

Afilar con—(This colloquialism has various meanings) : to court; to woo; to flirt; to be on the make; to make love (usually indicating an excess).

(1) Le gusta afilar con las muchachas.
He likes to woo the girls.
(Also used in Paraguay and Uruguay)

(2) Está afilando con Margarita.
He's flirting with Margaret. —or— He's on the make for Margaret.
(Also used in Paraguay and Uruguay)

Andar como bola sin manija—to be going around in circles (and not getting anything accomplished).

Anda como bola sin manija.
He's going around in circles.
(Also used in Paraguay and Uruguay)

Comer de arriba—to be a moocher.

Ese tipo come de arriba.
That fellow is a moocher.
(Also used in Paraguay and Uruguay)

[81]

Con bronca—begrudgingly; reluctantly.

Lo hizo con bronca.

He did it begrudgingly.
(Also used in Paraguay and Uruguay)

Darle el espiante—to give one the gate, or the air.

Su novia le dió el espiante.

His girl-friend gave him the air.
(Also used in Uruguay. Paraguay says it is "too Argentinian.")

Darse corte—to put on airs.

Se da mucho corte.

He puts on a lot of airs.
(Also used in Paraguay and Uruguay)

Darse dique—to put on airs.

Tu amigo se da mucho dique.

Your friend puts on a lot of airs.
(Also used in Uruguay)

Estar en cana—to be in the jug, or in jail.

Está en cana.

He's in the jug.

Estar en la vía—to be broke. (*finan.*)

Estoy en la vía.

I'm broke.

Estar entre San Juan y Mendoza—to be three sheets to the wind; to be swacked to the gills.

Está entre San Juan y Mendoza.

He's three sheets to the wind.

[82]

Gastar pólvora en chimangos—to waste one's ammunition, or efforts, on something not worthwhile.

No gastes pólvora en chimangos.
Don't waste your efforts on things that aren't worthwhile.

Hacer pito catalán—to thumb one's nose. (*ref. only to young children's antics*)

Lo ví haciendo pito catalán.
I saw him thumbing his nose.

> (NOTE: The action of thumbing one's nose in Spanish America is not vulgar—as in the U. S. A. Rather, the meaning approximates *our* expression, *Shame, shame!* —or— *Shame on you!*

Hacerle la pera—to stand one up (on a date or an appointment).

Tenía una cita con Alicia, y me hizo la pera.
I had a date with Alice, and she stood me up.
(Also used in Paraguay and Uruguay)

Hacerse el chancho rengo—to play dumb (in the sense of deliberately avoiding the issue, or deliberately ignoring what's going on around you).

No te hagas el chancho rengo.
Don't play dumb. (Don't avoid the issue.)
(Also popular in Paraguay and Uruguay)

Hacerse el otario—to play dumb. (*a little different idea than the above.* See example below.)

Cuando vino la policía me hice el otario.
When the police arrived, I played dumb.
(Also popular in Uruguay and Paraguay)

[83]

Hacerse la rabona—to play hooky.

> (NOTE: This colloquialism is generally used in the PAST tense, with either PAST or PRESENT significance.)

Se hizo la rabona.

He's playing hooky.   —or—   He played hooky.
(Also used in Paraguay and Uruguay)

Ir de farra   —or—   **farrear**—to go out on a spree; to go out and make whoopee.

> (NOTE: This colloquialism, while chiefly used in Argentina, has been adopted by many other South-American countries, especially those in the Río Plate area.)

Vamos de farra.   —OR—   Vamos a farrear.

Let's go out and make whoopee.

Ir de garufa—(Same as above, but used only in Argentina, Uruguay and Paraguay)

Meterle la mula—to gyp, or cheat, one.

Me metió la mula.

He gypped me.

Ni por un Perú—Not for all the money in the world. (*fig.*); Not for all the tea in China. (*fig.*)

(1) Used as a complete thought, as in the above phrase.
(2) No lo haría ni por un Perú.

> I wouldn't do it—not for all the tea in China.
> (Also used in Uruguay and Paraguay)

No tragarlo ni con bombilla de plata—not to be able to stand one; not to be able to stomach one.

No lo trago ni con bombilla de plata.

I can't stand him.

> (Also used in Uruguay)

Pasar el fardo—to pass the buck.

Me pasó el fardo.
He passed the buck to me.
(Paraguay and Uruguay use *echar* instead of **pasar**)

Quedarse sin el pan y sin la torta—to lose everything; to be left with nothing.
(Said of a person who, not satisfied with what he has, bargains for more and finally winds up by losing EVERYTHING. NOTE: Seems to be used only in the PAST TENSE.)

Se quedó sin el pan y sin la torta.
He (*or* she) wound up by losing everything.

Sobre el pucho—without hesitation; without a moment's delay; right away; right then and there.

Lo decidí sobre el pucho.
I decided on it right then and there.

BOLIVIA

Chacharse—to play hooky.

Los niños se están chachando.
The children are playing hooky.
(La Paz area)

(*Sp.*) **Darse mucho pisto**—to put on airs.

Aquella muchacha se da mucho pisto.
That girl puts on a lot of airs.
(Also used in Peru)

Hacerse el italiano—to play dumb.

¡No te hagas el italiano!
Don't play dumb.

Perder soga y cabrito—to lose everything; to be left with nothing.
> (Said of a person who, not satisfied with what he has, bargains for more and finally winds up by losing EVERYTHING. NOTE: Seems to be used only in the PAST TENSE.)

Perdió soga y cabrito.
He (*or* she) wound up by losing everything.

Quedarse con los crespos hechos—to be all dressed up and no place to go (implying a disappointment, or stand-up, at the last moment. When used by a man, this expression provokes laughter, as a man does not have *crespos*.)

Se quedó con los crespos hechos.
She was all dressed up and no place to go.
> (Also used in Chile and parts of Peru)

Rochearse—to play hooky.

Mañana me voy a rochear.
Tomorrow I'm going to play hooky.
> (Cochabamba area)

Tener "chaqui"—to have a hang-over.

Tengo "chaqui."
I have a hang-over.

[86]

Buscarle (el) cuesco a la breva—to look for trouble (*only* in the sense of looking for things that don't exist, or are impossible to find).

No le busque cuesco a la breva.
Don't look for trouble.

Cuando la perdiz críe cola—(This expression indicates that which is not likely to happen. An equivalent in English would be something along the lines of *When hell freezes over.*)

Estar cufifo—to be tipsy. (*applied to an alcoholic condition.*)

Estaba cufifo.
He was tipsy.

Hacer la cimarra—to play hooky.

Vamos a hacer la cimarra.
Let's play hooky.

Hacer la chancha—*See:* **hacer la cimarra.**

Levantarse el tarro—to talk a lot about oneself; to praise oneself a lot.

Se levanta el tarro.
He talks a lot about himself.
(Also used a little in Bolivia)

Pololear con—(This colloquialism has various meanings): to court; to woo; to flirt; to be on the make; to make love (usually indicating an excess).

(1) Me gusta pololear con las muchachas.
    I like to flirt with the girls.

[87]

(2) Tu amigo está pololeando con María.
Your friend is on the make for Mary.
(Also used in Bolivia)

Se armó la rosca—All Hell broke loose.

COLOMBIA

Amanecerá y veremos—Time will tell. —or— We'll see.

(This expression is frequently used for the purpose of
putting somebody off when a favor has been asked, in
which case it could be rendered as: *I'll let you know.*)
(Also used in Panama)

Capar (la) escuela—to play hooky.

Voy a capar (la) escuela.
I'm going to play hooky.

Cuando las gallinas críen dientes—(This expression indicates
that which is not likely to happen. An equivalent in English
would be something along the lines of *When hell freezes
over.*)

Estar como gato en una pelea de perros—to feel very uncomfortable, or out of place (at a party, in somebody's house,
etc.).

(Yo) estaba como gato en una pelea de perros.
I felt very uncomfortable. —or— I felt out of place.

Estar enguayabado—to have a hang-over.

Está enguayabado.
He has a hang-over.

[88]

Farsear con—to flirt (never really having serious intentions).

Juan farsea mucho con todas las muchachas.
John flirts a lot with all the girls.

(Sp.) Hacerse el inglés—to play dumb.

Se hizo el inglés.
He played dumb.

Ponerle bolas—to be attentive to one; to give one a tumble.

La ví en la calle, pero no me puso bolas.
I saw her on the street, but she didn't give me a tumble.

Ponerle pereque—to bother one.

¡No me ponga más pereque!
Don't bother me any more!

Ponerse la leva—(1) to play hooky. (2) to stay home from work.

(NOTE: This colloquialism is generally used in the PAST TENSE, with either PAST or PRESENT significance.)

Se puso la leva.
He's playing hooky. —or— He played hooky. —or— He stayed home from work.

Por la muerte de un obispo—Once in a blue moon.

(1) Used as a complete thought, as in the above phrase.
(2) La vemos por la muerte da un obispo.
We see her once in a blue moon.

(*Sp.*) Quedarse sin el pan y sin el perro—to lose everything; to be left with nothing.

(For a complete explanation, refer to **quedarse sin el pa 1 y sin la torta**—under Argentina.)

Se quedó sin el pan y sin el perro.
He (*or* she) wound up by losing everything.

COSTA RICA

Aventarse (de la escuela)—to play hooky.

(NOTE: This colloquialism is generally used in the PAST tense, with either PAST or PRESENT significance.)

Los niños se aventaron.
The children are playing hooky. —or— The children played hooky.

Caerle (como una) bala—to give one a pain in the neck. (*fig.*)

Esa mujer me cae (como una) bala.
That woman gives me a pain in the neck.
(Also used a little in Mexico, but NEVER OMIT *como una*)

Comer cuento—to take it all in (in the sense of believing what someone is telling you).

Está comiendo cuento.
He's taking it all in.

[90]

Cortarle el rabo—(1) to fire one (from a job); to give one the axe; to can one. (2) to give one his walking papers (either by the boss *or* the girl-friend.)

(1) Me cortaron el rabo.
They canned me. —or— I was fired.

(2) Mi novia me cortó el rabo.
My girl-friend gave me my walking papers.

Cuando la rana eche pelo (y el sapo rabo)—(This expression indicates that which is not likely to happen. An equivalent in English would be something along the lines of *When hell freezes over*.)

Dar cuerda—(This is a type of *street* flirting where either party, or both, will keep turning around several or more times, while walking along separately. There is no speech between them.)

La ví en la calle y le dí cuerda.
I saw her on the street and I flirted with her (*a la Costa Rica street style*).
(Also used in parts of Nicaragua)

Darle atolillo con el dedo—to kid, or string, one along.

Me está dando atolillo con el dedo.
He's stringing me along.

(*Sp.*) **Darse coba**—to brag about oneself; to give oneself an air of importance.

Se da mucha coba.
He sure brags enough about himself.
(Also used a little in Peru)

[91]

Dejarlo viendo para el ciprés—to stand one up (on a date or appointment).

Me dejaron viendo para el ciprés.
They stood me up.
(Also used in El Salvador)

Estar alzado—to be high, or tipsy. (*under the infl. of alcohol.*)
Está alzado.
He's high.
(Also used in Colombia)

Estar chonete—to be broke. (*finan.*)
Estoy chonete.
I'm broke.
(Also used *a little* in Nicaragua)

Estar en la jeruza—to be in the jug, or jail.
Está en la jeruza.
He's in the jug.
(While typically Costa-Rican, it is often used in Guatemala, El Salvador and Honduras)

Gastar pólvora en zopilote(s)—to waste one's ammunition, or efforts, on something not worthwhile.
No gastes pólvora en zopilote(s).
Don't waste your efforts on things that aren't worthwhile.
(Also used in Nicaragua)

Guardar el maíz del año—to save for a rainy day. (*fig.*)
Hay que guardar el maíz del año.
People should save for a rainy day.

Hacer película—to show off. —or— to be a show-off.

Hace mucha película.
He's quite a show-off.
  (Also used *a little* in Nicaragua)

Hacerse el chancho—to play dumb.

Se hizo el chancho.
He played dumb.
  (NOTE: This colloquialism is very popular but, because
  the word *chancho* is somewhat coarse, it should never
  be used in the presence of ladies, but rather among
  men intimates. However, it has no *immoral* connotation.)

Hacerse la rosita—to play hard to get. (*s.o. a girl only*)

Se hace la rosita.
She plays hard to get.

Ir de moscón—to go along as a chaperon.

Siempre que Anita sale con su novio, su hermana va de moscón.
Whenever Anita goes out with her boy-friend, her sister goes
 along as a chaperon.

Matar la culebra—to loaf; to kill time.

Está matando la culebra.
He's loafing.

No bajarlo ni con aceite—not to be able to stand one; not to be
 able to stomach one.

No lo bajo ni con aceite.
I can't stand him.
  (In Paraguay: *pasar* instead of **bajar**)

[93]

Parar la manta—to flee; to run away, but fast!; to up and leave in a big hurry.

Paró la manta.
He ran away, but fast! —or— He upped and left in a big hurry.

Patear el balde—to kick the bucket; to kick off; to die.

Hace dos días pateó el balde.
He kicked the bucket two days ago.
    (Also used in Honduras)

(*Sp.*) Quedarse sin el santo y sin la limosna—to lose everything; to be left with nothing.
    (For a complete explanation, refer to **quedarse sin el pan y sin la torta**—under Argentina.)

Se quedó sin el santo y sin la limosna.
He (*or* she) wound up by losing everything.
    (While chiefly used in Costa Rica, it is known in Nicaragua, Panama and Colombia. However, each of these countries has its own colloquialism to express the same idea—as will be found under each respective country.)

Quedarse sin Inés y sin (el) retrato—(Same as above, but somewhat less popular. Confined *only to Costa Rica.*)

Se quedó sin Inés y sin (el) retrato.
He (*or* she) wound up by losing everything.

Quedarse viendo para el ciprés—to be stood up (on a date, or appointment).

Se quedó viendo para el ciprés.
He (*or* she) was stood up.
    (Also used in El Salvador)

Si gustos no hubiera(n), en las tiendas no se vendiera(n)—
Everyone to his own taste.

¡Sigue Petra con calentura!—(This expression is used when a person persists in bringing up the same thing over and over again.)

    (1) There you go again with the same old stuff! (*when addressing a second person*)

    (2) There he (*or* she) goes again with the same old stuff! (*when speaking of a third person*)

¡Tan violeta!—My, how modest!

    (Used sarcastically or ironically—*meaning just the opposite*. Said of, or to, a person who talks a lot about himself or does a lot of bragging.)

Tener cabanga por—to be extremely homesick for; to miss very much.

Tengo cabanga por mi patria.

I'm very homesick for my native land.

    (Although chiefly used in Costa Rica, it is popular in Panama and Nicaragua)

¡Tumbe la vara!—Don't keep bothering me with that! —or— Lay off!

CUBA

"El País de la Ciguaraya"
The land where anything is possible

Coger un jalao—to get drunk.

Anoche cogió un jalao.
He got drunk last night.

[95]

Correrle la máquina—to kid, or string, one along.

Me estás corriendo la máquina.
You're stringing me along.

Chiflar el mono—to be extremely cold; to be cold as the dickens. (*s.o. the weather only*)

Chifla el mono-   —OR—   ¡Hace un frío que chifla el mono!
It's cold as the dickens.

Darle cranque—(This colloquialism is difficult to render as an equivalent in English. It suggests giving one a verbal push to get him started, in order to make him do or say something that he does not wish to.)

Hay que darle cranque.
You have to give him a push.

Darse lija—to put on airs.

Se da mucha lija.
He (*or* she) puts on a lot of airs.

.(*Sp.*) **De Pascuas a San Juan**—Once in a blue moon.

(1) Used as a complete thought, as in the above phrase.

(2) Lo veo de Pascuas a San Juan.
I see him once in a blue moon.

Donde el diablo dió los tres gritos (or **las tres voces**)— Way out to Hell-'n'-gone.

(1) Used as a complete thought, as in the above phrase.

(2) Tu casa queda donde el diablo dió los tres gritos.
Your house is way out to Hell-'n'-gone.

(NOTE: In Spain, substitute *Cristo* for **el diablo**, and use
las tres voces.)

Estar en la fuácata—to be flat broke. (*finan.*)

Estoy en la fuácata.
I'm flat broke.
(Also used in Veracruz, Mexico)

Estar en la prángana—*Same as above*

Está en la prángana.
He's flat broke.
(Also used in parts of Mexico)

Futigarse —or— **Futivarse**—to play hooky.
(NOTE: This colloquialism is generally used in the PAST
tense, with either PAST or PRESENT significance.)

Se futigó. —OR— Se futivó.
He played hooky.
—or—
He's playing hooky.
(Used only in parts of Cuba)

Ir de cumbancha—to go out on a bender.

Anoche fuimos de cumbancha.
Last night we went out on a bender.

Irse de rumba—to go out for a good time.

Vámonos de rumba.
Let's go out for a good time.

[97]

¡Le zumba el mango!—(An expression indicating that a person or thing has lots of *it* or *oomph;* is *strictly in the groove* or *the last word*. While Cuban in origin, it is getting around quite a bit. It is frequently used in Panama, Costa Rica, and parts of Mexico—and crops up now and then in various other countries of Central America.)

¡Ni de jarana!—I wouldn't dream of it! —or— Not on your life!

No tener ni un kilo—to be flat broke; not to have a penny.

No tengo ni un kilo.
I'm flat broke.

(Sp.) **Pegar la gorra**—to sponge.

Vino a pegarme la gorra.
He came to sponge on me.

Pelar la guásima—to play hooky.

Está pelando la guásima.
He's playing hooky.
(Used only in parts of Cuba)

Quedarse vestido y sin bailar—to be all dressed up and no place to go. (implying a disappointment, or stand-up, at the last moment)

Se quedó vestida y sin bailar.
She was all dressed up and no place to go.

Saber nadar sin mojarse la ropa—(s.o. a person who is clever and knows how to keep himself in the clear, without getting caught.)

Sabe nadar sin mojarse la ropa.
He's the kind of a guy who knows how to stay in the clear, and never gets caught.

(NOTE: In Spain: *Saber nadar y guardar la ropa*)

¡Se formó el rollo!—All Hell broke loose!

¡Se formó / armó **el titingó!**—*Same as above.*

Ser un buche y pluma—(Said of a person who is a big bluff)

Es un buche y pluma.
He's a big bluff.

(NOTE: This expression has been taken from an old Cuban folk-song entitled "Buche y Pluma N'Má." The first three words are pronounced as if they were written *boo-chee-plu-mah.*)

Tirarse un papelazo—to make oneself ridiculous.

Se tiró un papelazo anoche en la reunión.
He made himself ridiculous at the party last night.

(*Sp.*) Vivir en las quimbambas—to be from, or live way out in, the sticks.

Vive en las quimbambas.

He's from the sticks. —or— He lives way out in the sticks.

[99]

ECUADOR

¡Anda a quejarte a un belermo!—(This expression is used to shut a person up who is complaining.) An approximation in English would be along the lines of:

I don't want to hear your troubles! —or— I *told* you so!

Armar boche—to start a fight; to start trouble.

Armó boche.
He started a fight.

Buscar chivo—to look for trouble.

El siempre está buscando chivo.
He's always looking for trouble.

Comer (or **vivir**) **de pavo**—to sponge; to be a sponger, or a parasite.

Come de pavo.
He's a sponger. —or— He's a parasite.

Chumarse—to get drunk.

Esta noche me voy a chumar.
Tonight I'm going to get drunk.

Echar hoja—to play hooky.

Vamos a echar hoja.
Let's play hooky.

Estar empavado—to be out of sorts.

Está empavado.
He's out of sorts.

(NOTE: In Peru, *empavado* means *blushing*)

Estar en (una) ráfaga—to be broke. (*finan.*)

Estoy en (una) ráfaga.
I'm broke.

Hacerle chino—to fool one.

Trató de hacerme chino.
He tried to fool me.
(Also used in Peru)

Por la muerte de un judío—Once in a blue moon.

(1) Used as a complete thought, as in the above phrase.

(2) Lo veo por la muerte de un judío.
I see him once in a blue moon.

Quedarse con las narices largas—to have a big let-down; to be disappointed.

Se quedaron con las narices largas.
They had a big let-down. —or— They were disappointed.

Quedarse sin pan ni pedazo—to lose everything; to be left with nothing.
(For a complete explanation, refer to **quedarse sin el pan y sin la torta**—under Argentina.)

Se quedó sin pan ni pedazo.
He (*or* she) wound up by losing everything.
(Also used in Chile)

Tener un chuchaqui ⎱
    —or— ⎰ —to have a hang-over.
Estar con chuchaqui

Tengo un chuchaqui. —OR— Estoy con chuchaqui.
I have a hang-over.   I have a hang-over.

EL SALVADOR

A todo cuche se le llega su sábado—(This philosophical expression, generally used in a sarcastic sense, arises from the fact that in many of the Central-American republics, the people who live in the villages slaughter the pigs on Saturday.)

(1) One of these days you'll get what's coming to you. (*when addressing a second person*)

(2) Everybody gets what's coming to him—sooner or later. (*when speaking generally, or of a third person*)

Apachar el clavo—to mooch. (usually taking advantage of a given situation to do so)

Invité a Juan a tomar una copa, y vino Alberto a apacharme el clavo.

I invited John to have a drink, and along came Albert to mooch one for himself.

Caerle en la nuca—to give one a pain in the neck. (*fig.*)

Me cae en la nuca.

He (*or* she) gives me a pain in the neck.

(Also used in parts of Guatemala and Honduras)

Doblar el caite—to kick the bucket; to cash in one's chips; to die.

Está para doblar el caite.

He's just about ready to cash in his chips.

¡Échele maíz a la chumpa!—Come on, get going! Get moving! Give out! (This expression is generally used to incite a person into doing or telling something. A *literal* translation in English would have little or no meaning to us.)

Estar en la real quema—to be flat broke. (*finan.*)

Estoy en la real quema.

I'm flat broke.
> (While typical of El Salvador, it is frequently used in Guatemala, Honduras and Nicaragua)

Gastar pólvora en zope(s)—to waste one's ammunition, or efforts, on something not worthwhile.

No gastes pólvora en zopes.

Don't waste your efforts on things that aren't worthwhile.

Hacerse el del ojo pacho—to pretend not to notice; to look the other way.
> (Same as **hacerse de la vista gorda**—under PART II)

Se hizo el del ojo pacho.

He pretended not to notice. —or— He looked the other way.

Hacerse el papo—to play dumb.

No te hagas el papo.

Don't play dumb.
> (Also used in Guatemala)

Hacerse la "Greta"—to play hard to get.
> (The "Greta" part alludes to Miss Garbo.)

Está haciéndose la "Greta."

She's playing hard to get.

¡Hay pericos en la milpa (y loras en las estacas)!—Jiggers!
> —or— The coast is not clear!
> (Either element of the phrase may be used separately—or the entire phrase jointly.)
> (Also used in Guatemala)

Liar el petate—to kick the bucket; to kick off; to die.

Lió el petate.
He kicked the bucket.
(Also used a little in Guatemala and parts of Mexico)

No pasarlo ni envuelto en huevo—not to be able to stand one; not to be able to stomach one.

No lo paso ni envuelto en huevo.
I can't stand him.
(Also used a little in Guatemala)

Quedarse con los colochos hechos—to be all dressed up and no place to go (implying a disappointment, or stand-up, at the last moment. When used by a man, this expression provokes laughter, as a man does not have *colochos.*)

Se quedó con los colochos hechos.
She was all dressed up and no place to go.

Sentirse (or **estar**) **como pollo comprado**—to feel out of place (at somebody's house, at a party, gathering, etc.)

Me siento (estoy) como pollo comprado.
I feel out of place.
(While typical of El Salvador, it is also used in Honduras and parts of Guatemala)

Tener cuello—to have a lot of pull, drag, or influence.

Mi hermano tiene cuello.
My brother has a lot of pull.
(Also used in Guatemala)

GUATEMALA

A todo coche se le llega su sábado—(This philosophical expression, generally used in a sarcastic sense, arises from the fact that in many of the Central-American republics, the people who live in the villages slaughter the pigs on Saturday.)

(1) One of these days you'll get what's coming to you. (*when addressing a second person*)

(2) Everybody gets what's coming to him—sooner or later. (*when speaking generally, or of a third person*)

Agarrarlo con la gallina bajo el brazo—to catch one red-handed; to catch one with the goods; to catch one in the act (of doing something he shouldn't).

Lo agarramos con la gallina bajo el brazo.
We caught him with the goods.
(Also used a little in El Salvador)

Darse paquete—to put on airs.

Se dan mucho paquete.
They put on a lot of airs.
(Also used in Mexico)

Gastar pólvora en sanate(s)—to waste one's ammunition, or efforts, on something not worthwhile.

No gastes pólvora en sanate(s).
Don't waste your efforts on things that aren't worthwhile.

Hacerse el peje—to play dumb.

No te hagas el peje.
Don't play dumb.
(Also used in El Salvador)

[105]

Hacerse el sapo—to play dumb.

Me hice el sapo.
I played dumb.
(In El Salvador, *sapito* is used)

No pasarlo ni con tragos de agua de brasa—not to be able to stand one; not to be able to stomach one.

No la paso ni con tragos de agua de brasa.
I can't stand her.

Patear la cubeta—to kick the bucket; to kick off; to die.

Pateó la cubeta.
He kicked the bucket.

Quedarse sin el mico y sin la montera—to lose everything; to be left with nothing.
(For a complete explanation, refer to **quedarse sin el pan y sin la torta**—under Argentina.)

Se quedó sin el mico y sin la montera.
He (*or* she) wound up by losing everything.

HONDURAS

Caerle como píldora—to give one a pain in the neck. (*fig.*)

Me cae como píldora.
He (*or* she) gives me a pain in the neck.

Gastar pólvora en tincutes—to waste one's ammunition, or efforts, on something not worthwhile.

No gastes pólvora en tincutes.
Don't waste your efforts on things that aren't worthwhile.

Hacer zócalo—(s.o. a girl when she is not invited to dance, at a party, gathering, etc. Hence, *to be a wallflower* —or— *to sit out every dance*.)

Hizo zócalo toda la noche.

She sat out every dance, all evening long.
—or—
She was a wallflower.

¡Hay (moros en la costa y) pericos en la montaña!—Jiggers!
—or— The coast is not clear!

No pasarlo ni con candelas / ni en galleta — not to be able to stand, or bear one; not to be able to stomach one.

No lo paso ni con candelas (*or* ni en galleta).

I can't stand him.
(Also used a little in Nicaragua, but: *no pasarlo ni con candelas*)

Pagar los elotes—(1) to get the blame, or suffer the consequences, for something you haven't done.
(2) to be left holding the bag.

Yo pagué los elotes.

I got the blame (and suffered the consequences).
—or—
I was left holding the bag.
(Also popular in Nicaragua)

(*Sp.*) **Quedarse compuesta y sin novio**—to be stood up. (s.o. a girl, dressed and made up for her date, whose boy-friend doesn't show up.)

Se quedó compuesta y sin novio.

She was stood up.
(Also used in Peru, and a little in El Salvador)

Quedarse sin el plato y sin la cena—to lose everything; to be left with nothing.
(For a complete explanation, refer to **Quedarse sin el pan y sin la torta**—under Argentina.)

Se quedó sin el plato y sin la cena.
He (*or* she) wound up by losing everything.
(Also very popular in El Salvador)

Tener golilla—to have pull, drag, or influence.

Hay que tener golilla.
You have to have pull.

MEXICO

A cada capillita se le llega su fiestecita—(An approximate equivalent would be something along the lines of *Every dog has his day.*)

(*Sp.*) ¡Ahí está el detalle!—That's the point!

(NOTE: With the advent of Cantinflas, famous Mexican comic, many new expressions have been born, and old ones popularized. The above is one of his pet phrases which he will deliberately insert in his rapid-fire dialogue, whether it fits the occasion or not. The expression is also gaining ground in many places, outside of Mexico, where Cantinflas' films are shown.)

Ahora es cuando—*Now* is the time! *Now* is your chance!
(Although really a Mexicanism, it is gaining popularity in Central America. It is well known in Guatemala.)

[108]

¡**Así, sí baila mi hija con el señor!**—(This expression is used when you agree with a person, or when he finally meets your terms.) An equivalent would be:

Now you're talking! —or— *Now* you're making sense!

¡**Barbas tienes!**—(This expression is capable of many interpretations—*all sarcastic*—along the lines of *Phooey!—Who are you trying to kid?—Are you trying to kid me?—You're all wet!*—etc.)

Ana: —Yo nunca engaño a mi marido.
María: —¡Barbas tienes, mi hijita!

Anna: I never deceive my husband.
Mary: Who are you trying to kid, honey?

    (NOTE: *mi hijita* is pronounced rapidly—as if it were spelled *mijita*)

Cada Corpus y San Juan—Once in a blue moon.

(1) Used as a complete thought, as above.

(2) Pasa por aquí cada Corpus y San Juan.
He comes by here once in a blue moon.

Caerle gordo—to give one a pain in the neck. (*fig.*)

Me cae gordo.	Me cae gorda.
He gives me a pain in the neck.	She gives me a pain in the neck.

Caerle sangrón—*Same as above.*

Me cae sangrón.	Me cae sangrona.
He gives me a pain in the neck.	She gives me a pain in the neck.

[109]

Caerse muerto (or **cadáver**)—to pay up; to come across; to cough up. (*fig.*)

(Seems to be used as a command only)

¡Cáete muerto! —OR— ¡Cáete cadáver!

Come across! Pay up! Cough up!

(The above expression is also very popular in Guatemala, where the reflexive is generally omitted and *cadáver* seems to be preferred, e.g., *¡Cae cadáver!*)

¡Con dinero baila el chango! el perro! —Money talks!

Creerse la divina garza—to think oneself quite the thing; to be stuck up.

Se cree la divina garza.

He thinks himself quite the thing.

Darle atole con el dedo—to kid, or string, one along.

No me des atole con el dedo.

Don't string me along.

Echar a uno de cabeza—to tell on one (in the sense of *giving one away*).

No me eches de cabeza.

Don't tell on me.

Echarle la viga—to give one Hell; to give one the dickens; to bawl one out.

Me echó la viga.

He gave me the dickens.

En gustos se rompen géneros—Everyone to his own taste.

[110]

Entre azul y buenas noches—undecided; unsettled. (*s.o. a situation*)

Juan: —Tu libro, ¿cuándo lo van a publicar?
Pedro: —Bueno . . . la cosa está entre azul y buenas noches.

John: When are they going to publish your book?
Peter: Well, the whole thing is still pretty much undecided.

¡Está piocha (or **repiocha**)!—(s.o. persons or things that are excellent or magnificent. An equivalent in English would be *It's super-duper!* —or— *He (or she) is super!*)

Juanita: —¿Qué (tal) le pareció Ronald Colman?
Carmen: —¡Está (re)piocha!

Jane: What did you think of Ronald Colman?
Carmen: He's super!
   (NOTE: In uttering this expression, rub your chin in a downward motion, as if you were stroking a goatee.)

¡Está tres piedras!—*Same meaning as above*
   (While Mexican in origin, it is well known throughout Central America. In Guatemala, they frequently embellish it by adding *y un tetunte*. In Mexico, quite often, *y un tepeyahualco*. In uttering this expression, form a circle with your thumb and index finger, thereby keeping the remaining three fingers aloft. Now, raise your arm to about shoulder level, or a little above, and give the hand a slight jerk.)

Estar bruja—to be broke. (*finan.*)

Estoy bruja.
I'm broke.
   (Also popular in Cuba)

   (NOTE: *bruja*, although ending in an *a*, is the same in both genders.)

Estar crudo—to have a hang-over.

Estamos crudos.
We have a hang-over.
   (Also used in Cuba)

Estar cuete—to be tipsy or tight. (*app. to an alcoholic condition*)

Está cuete.
He's tipsy.

Estar en el bote—to be in the jug, or in jail.

Está en el bote.
He's in the jug.

Estar en la (quinta) chilla—to be down and out; to be flat broke; not to have a penny to one's name.

Estoy en la (quinta) chilla.
I'm down and out. —or— I'm flat broke. —or— I haven't a penny to my name.

Estar en su mero mole—to be right in one's element; to be right where one belongs.

Margarita: —¿Sabes que tu esposo está en la cantina, tomando con sus amigos?

Dolores: —¡Hum! Está en su mero mole.

Margaret: Do you know your husband's in the saloon, drinking with his friends?

Dolores: Hmm! He's right in his element.

[112]

Gastar (la) pólvora en infiernitos—to waste one's ammunition, or efforts on something not worthwhile.

No gastes pólvora en infiernitos.
Don't waste your efforts on things that aren't worthwhile.

Hacer a uno de chivo los tamales—(1) to double-cross; to make a sucker out of one; to put something over on one. (2) to cheat. (in the above sense, *or on one's husband*)

(1) Me hizo de chivo los tamales.
He double-crossed me.
—or—
He put one over on me.
—or—
He made a sucker out of me.
(Also used in Guatemala)

(2) Su esposa le está haciendo de chivo los tamales.
His wife is cheating on him.
(Also used in Guatemala)

Hacerle la barba—to polish the apple; to play up to one.

Te está haciendo la barba.
He's playing up to you.
—or—
He's polishing the apple.

(NOTE: When using this colloquialism, rub your right cheek up and down with the back of your right hand, using the lower part of the hand.)

Hacerle la llorona—to give one a sob-story.

Le hice la llorona y me dió dos pesos.
I gave him a sob-story and he gave me two pesos.

[113]

Hacerse guaje—to play dumb.

No te hagas guaje.
Don't play dumb.

Hacerse para atrás—to back out. (*fig.*)

Prometió ayudarme, pero se hizo para atrás.
He promised to help me, but he backed out.
(Also used in Guatemala)

(NOTE: For other countries, including Spain, use *echarse* in place of **hacerse**.)

Hacerse pato—to play dumb.

¡Hazte pato, que aquí vienen los cuicos
Play dumb! Here come the cops!

Irse de mosca—(1) to bum one's way; not to pay one's fare.
(2) to go as a stowaway.

(NOTE: This colloquialism is generally used in the PAST TENSE.)

Se fué de mosca.
He bummed his way. —or— He went as a stowaway.

Irse de pinta—to play hooky.

(NOTE: This colloquialism is generally used in the PAST tense, with either PAST or PRESENT significance.)

Se fué de pinta.
He's playing hooky. —or— He played hooky.

[114]

¡La cosa está color de hormiga!—It looks pretty bad! Things are getting pretty hot! (indicating that the situation is tense, serious or dangerous.)

> (NOTE: Although used chiefly in Mexico, it is also popular in Cuba, Guatemala and El Salvador.)

¡La vida no vale tres cacahuates!—Life isn't worth a darn! Life isn't worth living!

Llevar (or **dar**) **gallo**—to serenade.

Le llevo (doy) gallo todas las noches.
I serenade her every night.

Mientras (or **entre**) **menos burros, más olotes**—(fam. exp. pointing up the advantage of having just a *few* people in attendance, so that the remainder may benefit more fully themselves by the absence of the others. Often said when a person declines a dinner invitation, or some special plate.) An equivalent in English would be:

The fewer the better! —or— *The less people, the more we have to eat!*

Pellar gallo—(1) to take a powder; to fly the coop; to skip; to scram.
　　　　　　(2) VERY INFREQUENTLY: to kick the bucket; to die.

> (NOTE: Almost always used in the PAST TENSE.)

Peló gallo.
He flew the coop. —or— He scrammed.

Pelarse de casquete—*Same as above.*

Se peló de casquete.
He took a powder. —or— He skipped.

[115]

Peor es chile y el agua lejos—It's never so bad but that it couldn't be worse.

> (NOTE: In pronouncing this expression, the *e* of the *el* is dropped, and *el agua* sounds as if it were written *l'agua*.)

¡Pícale!—Step on it! Hurry up! Get a move on!

Pintar venado—to play hooky.

> (NOTE: This colloquialism is generally used in the PAST tense, with either PAST or PRESENT significance.)

Pintó venado.

He's playing hooky. —or— He played hooky.

Pintarle un violín—to make one a promise and not keep it; to deceive one.

Me pintó un violín.

He made me a promise and he didn't keep it. —or— He deceived me.

Ponerle los ojos verdes—to try to pull the wool over one's eyes (by telling one a lot of trumped-up stories).

Me puso los ojos verdes.

He tried to pull the wool over my eyes.

Ponerse chango—to be alert; to be on one's toes.

> (NOTE: This colloquialism seems to be used mostly as a command, in the familiar.)

¡Ponte chango!

Be on your toes! Be alert!

¡**Por ahí va la bola!**—That's the way the wind is blowing! (*fig.*)

—or—

That's the general idea!

(This expression is frequently used when one doesn't feel like going into detail about a particular thing, or doesn't wish to divulge fully some information. The *ahí* is generally pronounced as if it were written *ay*, and is often spelled this way.)

(*Sp.*) ¡**Por si las moscas . . . !**—Just in case!

(Another of Cantinflas' pet phrases. It is, and should always be, used among intimate friends. Has no immoral connotation.)

Pepe: —¿Por qué usas pistola?
Carlitos: —¡Por si las moscas . . . !

Joe: Why are you carrying a gun?
Charlie: Just in case!

Quedarse como el que chifló en la loma—to be left high and dry. (*fig.*); to be left out in the cold. (*fig.*)

Me quedé como el que chifló en la loma.

I was left high and dry. —or— I was left out in the cold.

Quedarse sin Juan y sin las gallinas—to lose everything; to be left with nothing.

(For a complete explanation, refer to **quedarse sin el pan y sin la torta**—under Argentina.)

Se quedó sin Juan y sin las gallinas.

He (*or* she) wound up by losing everything.

[117]

Rajarse—to back out; to get cold feet. (*fig.*)

Se rajó.

He backed out. —or— He got cold feet.
(Also used in Cuba, Guatemala and El Salvador)
(NOTE: In Honduras, Costa Rica and Panama, **rajarse**
means *to treat; to pay the check.*)

Juan se rajó.   Pedro se rajó con las copas.

John treated.   Peter treated to the drinks.

—or—

John paid the check.

Saber lo que es amar a Dios en tierra ajena—to have experi-
enced hardships through lack of friends or resources; to
know what it means to suffer (in the generic sense).

Yo sé lo que es amar a Dios en tierra ajena.

I know what it means to suffer.

(NOTE: Does not have to refer to a *foreign land.*)

Ser buena reata—to be a good sport; to be a regular guy.

Es buena reata.

He's a good sport. —or— He's a regular guy.
(In Guatemala and El Salvador: *pura reata*, which also
has the meaning of *daring* or *brave.*)

Ser un águila descalza—to be a darn clever chap. (usually in
the sense that nobody can put anything over on you)

Es un águila descalza.

He's a darn clever chap.

(*Sp.*) **Tenerlo en salmuera**—to have one on the spot; to have
one right where you want him.

[118]

Lo tengo en salmuera.
I have him on the spot.

Tirarle plancha—to stand one up (on a date or appointment).

Me tiró plancha.
He (*or* she) stood me up.

Tragar camote—to swallow hard; to have to take it. (*fig.*); not
to be able to answer.

El jefe me regañó y yo tragué camote.
The boss bawled me out and I had to take it.

Volteársele a uno el chirrión por el palito—to have something
back-fire on one.

Se le volteó el chirrión por el palito.
It back-fired on him.
> (Exactly the same as **salirle el tiro por la culata**—under
> PART II. Please refer to same for a more complete
> idea as to how this colloquialism may be used in a given
> situation.)

Ya ni llorar es bueno—Don't cry over spilt milk.

¡Ya tengo colmillo(s)!—I've been around! —or— I wasn't
born yesterday!
> (NOTE: In uttering this expression, tap an eye-tooth with
> one of your fingers.)

¡Yo Colón y mis hijos Cristobalitos!—You don't have to tell me!
—or— I already know about that!
(In Guatemala, it is generally shortened, or changed, to *¡Ya
Colón!*)

NICARAGUA

Cada lora a (or **en**) **su guanacaste**—Everyone in his (own) place.

Comer pato—(s.o. a girl when she is not invited to dance, at a party, gathering, etc. Hence, *to be a wallflower* —or— *to sit out every dance*.)

Comió pato toda la noche.
She sat out every dance, the entire evening.
—or—
She was a wallflower.

Darle picones—to tease one by making him, or her, jealous. (*applied to novios*)

María le está dando picones.
Mary is making him jealous.
—or—
Mary is teasing him.
(Also very popular in Mexico)

Dejarlo viendo para el icaco—to stand one up (on a date or appointment).

Me dejó viendo para el icaco.
He (*or* she) stood me up.

¡Échele chicha al cumbo!—Keep it going! Keep it alive!

Estarle a uno arañando el tigre—to be extremely hungry; to be so hungry you could eat a horse.

¡Me está arañando el tigre!
I'm so hungry I could eat a horse!
(Also very popular in Panama)

[120]

Hacer de una aguja un machete—to make a mountain out of a mole-hill. (*fig.*)

Estás haciendo de una aguja un machete.
You're making a mountain out of a mole-hill.

Hacerse la flor—to make oneself important, or to play hard to get. (*s.o. a girl only*)

Se hace la flor.
She plays hard to get. —or— She makes herself important.

¡Hay (moros en la costa y) pericos en la loma!—Jiggers!
—or— The coast is not clear!

Pelar el ajo—to kick the bucket; to kick off; to die.

Peló el ajo.
He kicked the bucket.

Quedarse sin Beatriz y sin retrato—to lose everything; to be left with nothing.
   (For a complete explanation, refer to **quedarse sin el pan y sin la torta**—under Argentina.)

Se quedó sin Beatriz y sin retrato.
He (*or* she) wound up by losing everything.
   (Also used a little in Honduras)

Quedarse viendo para el icaco—to be stood up (on a date or appointment).

Me quedé viendo para el icaco.
I was stood up.

[121]

Sentirse (or **estar**) **como gallina comprada**—to feel out of place (at somebody's house, at a party, gathering, etc.).

Me siento (estoy) como gallina comprada.
I feel out of place.
(Also used in Guatemala)

PANAMA

¡Cógelo suave!—Take it easy!

Comer del cuento—to fall for it (in the sense of believing what someone tells you).

Le dije que Juan tenía dos hijos, y comió del cuento.
I told him John had two children, and he fell for it.

Estar en la chirola—to be in the jug, or in jail.

Está en la chirola.
He's in the jug.
> (*Chirola* is also used in those parts of Costa Rica that are influenced more by Panama's proximity than by Nicaragua's. *Chirona,* without the article, is substituted for *chirola* principally in Nicaragua; also Honduras, Guatemala, El Salvador, and those parts of Costa Rica that are influenced more by Nicaragua's proximity than by Panama's—in which case Costa Rica generally uses *chirona* in the following way:

(*Sp.*) Se lo llevaron a la chirona.
They took him away to jail.

[122]

While principally used in Central America, *chirona* has become popular in Mexico and Peru. Chile also uses *chirona* in the following way:

(*Sp.*) Lo metieron en chirona.
They put him in jail.
—or—
They threw him in the jug.

Estar en fuego—to be drunk; to be lit. (*fig.*)

Está en fuego.
He's lit.

Estar limpio de bola—to be broke. (*finan.*)

Estoy limpio de bola.
I'm broke.

Estar matado—*Same as above.*

Estoy matado.
I'm broke.

Estar traqueado—to be tight, or tipsy. (*under the infl. of alcohol*)

Está traqueado.
He's tight.

Ganarse un camarón—to make a little extra money on the side.

¿Quieres ganarte un camarón?
Do you want to make a little extra money on the side?
(While typically Panamanian, it is also popular in Costa Rica and Nicaragua)

Ir a la alemana—to go Dutch treat.

Vamos a la alemana.
Let's go Dutch.

Meterle un cují—to cheat; to gyp; to put something over on one.
(especially applied to dealings with money)

Me metió un cují.
He cheated me. —or— He put one over on me. —or— He gypped me.

Pavearse—to play hooky.
(NOTE: This colloquialism is generally used in the PRESENT PERFECT tense, to denote a present progressive action.)

(1) Se han paveado.
They are playing hooky.

(2) Mañana me voy a pavear.
Tomorrow I'm going to play hooky.

Quedarse con el pecado y sin el género—to lose everything; to be left with nothing.
(For a complete explanation, refer to **quedarse sin el pan y sin la torta**—under Argentina.)

Se quedó con el pecado y sin el género.
He (*or* she) wound up by losing everything.
(Also used in Colombia)

Se armó el lerelere—All Hell broke loose.
(Used mostly in the *interior* of Panama)

Si los gustos fueran iguales, las telas no se venderían—Everyone to his own taste.

[124]

PARAGUAY

(*Sp.*) **Caerle como un rayo**—to give one a pain in the neck. (*fig.*)

Me cae como un rayo.
He (*or* she) gives me a pain in the neck.

Comer de upa—to be a moocher.

Ese tipo come de upa.
That guy is a moocher.

En todas partes se queman las papas—That can happen any-where; It happens in the best of families.
(Same as **En todas partes cuecen habas**—under PART III)

Hacer de Tomasito—to butt in (on a pair of lovers).

No quiero hacer de Tomasito.
I don't want to butt in on them.

Hacer la "ere"—to play hooky.

(NOTE: This colloquialism is generally used in the PAST tense, with either PAST or PRESENT significance. In Paraguay, **"ere"** is short for *rabona,* and is probably more common than the latter, among school children.)

Hizo la "ere."
He's playing hooky. —or— He played hooky.

No poder ver a uno ni en caja de fósforos—not to be able to stand, or bear, one.

No lo puedo ver ni en caja de fósforos.
I can't bear him.
(Also used in Uruguay, and some parts of Argentina)

Ponerle el canasto—to pass the buck.

Me puso el canasto.
He passed the buck to me.

Tener olor a leche—to be very young; to be still a baby. (*s.o. a girl*)

Esa muchacha es muy joven para mí. Tiene olor a leche.
That girl is too young for me. She's still a baby.

PERU

¡A otro burro con esa carga!—Give it to somebody else!
—or—
Don't bother me with that!
(Also used a little in parts of Ecuador and Colombia)

Comerse un pavo—to blush.

Se comió un pavo.
He (*or* she) blushed.

Cuando los pollos mamen, y cuando los sastres hagan chalecos con mangas—
(This expression indicates, of course, that which is not likely to happen. An equivalent in English would be something along the lines of *When hell freezes over*. Either element of the phrase may be used separately, or the entire phrase jointly.)

Decirle vela verde—to be brutally insulting to one; to tell one where to head in, or where to get off.

Le dije vela verde.
I really told him where to get off.
(Also used in Ecuador)

Empavarse—to blush.

Cuando traté de besarla, se empavó.

When I tried to kiss her, she blushed.

Estar como gallina en corral ajeno—to feel out of place (at somebody's house, at a party, gathering, etc.).

Estoy como gallina en corral ajeno.

I feel out of place.
(Also used in Colombia)

Estar con la perseguidora—to have a hang-over.

Estoy con la perseguidora.

I have a hang-over.

Estarle a uno corriendo el león—to be extremely hungry; to be so hungry you could eat a horse.

¡Me está corriendo el león!

I'm so hungry I could eat a horse!

Guardar pan para mayo—to save for a rainy day. (*fig.*)

Hay que guardar pan para mayo.

One should save for a rainy day.

Hacer teatro—to try to appear big; to try to impress.

Está haciendo teatro.

He's trying to appear big.
                —or—
He's trying to impress.
(Also used in Bolivia, and a little in Chile)

[127]

Hacerse la vaca—to play hooky.

(Se) está haciendo la vaca.	Se hizo la vaca.
He's playing hooky.	He played hooky.

Ir de jarana —or— **jaranear**—to go out on a spree; to go out and make merry.

Anoche fuimos de jarana.
Last night we went out on a spree.

Vamos a jaranear.
Let's go out and make merry.
   (While typical of Peru, it is also popular in Bolivia and Colombia. Less common in Argentina, Chile and Ecuador)

Largarlo tieso—to tell one to go to Hell (in the sense of turning one down abruptly).

Lo largué tieso.
I told him to go to Hell.   —or—   I turned him down—but abruptly!

Pedir el sol por salir—to ask the impossible; to ask for an awful lot.

Estás pidiendo el sol por salir.
You're asking the impossible.

Perder soga y cabra
      —or—
Quedarse sin la soga y sin la cabra }—to lose everything; to be left with nothing.
   (For a complete explanation, refer to **quedarse sin el pan y sin la torta**—under Argentina.)

Perdió soga y cabra.   —OR—   Se quedó sin la soga y sin la cabra.
He (or she) wound up by losing everything.

[128]

Ponerse pije—to get all dolled up (in a loud or flashy manner).

Se puso pije.
He got all dolled up.
(Also used in Bolivia and parts of Chile)

Ser un "chicheñor"—to be a yes-man.

Es un "chicheñor."
He's a yes-man.

Sobarle la pantorrilla—to polish the apple; to play up to one.

Me está sobando la pantorrilla.
He's polishing the apple. —or— He's playing up to me.

Tirar prosa—(1) to give oneself an air of importance; to play the big shot.
(2) to do a lot of bragging.

(1) Le gusta tirar prosa.
He likes to play the big shot.

(2) Tira mucha prosa.
He does a lot of bragging.
(Also used in Ecuador. In Bolivia: *tirarse* prosa)

Verle las orejas al galgo—not to have enough to eat (in the sense of poverty).

Hace muy poco tiempo, le veía las orejas al galgo.
A short time ago, he didn't have enough to eat.

[129]

Hacerlo largar el hueso—to make one confess.

Lo hice largar el hueso.
I made him confess.

Hacerse la pelada—to play hooky.

(NOTE: This colloquialism is generally used in the PAST tense, with either PAST or PRESENT significance.)

Se hizo la pelada.
He's playing hooky. —or— He played hooky.

Tirársela de perro lanudo—to brag, or to go around trying to give the impression that you have more than you really do— or that you are better off than you really are.

Se la tira de perro lanudo.
He goes around trying to give the impression he's better off than he really is.

Agarrarlo con el queso en la mano—to catch one red-handed; to catch one with the goods; to catch one in the act (of doing something he shouldn't).

Lo agarré con el queso en la mano.
I caught him red-handed.

Cuando al sapo le salgan pelos y al lagartijo copete—(This expression indicates, of course, that which is not likely to happen. An equivalent in English would be something along the lines of *When hell freezes over.*)

Estar como cucaracha en baile de gallinas—to be neglected and feel out of place (at somebody's house, at a party, gathering, dance, etc.).

En la reunión de anoche estuve como cucaracha en baile de gallinas.
I was neglected and felt out of place at the party last night.

Estar en la carraplana—to be in a tough spot.

Estoy en la carraplana desde que los salteadores me robaron el dinero.
I'm in a tough spot since the highwaymen robbed me of my money.

Estar enratonado⎱
　　—or—　　⎰—to have a hang-over.
Tener un ratón⎰

Estoy enratonado.　—OR—　Tengo un ratón.
I have a hang-over.

Estar vitoqueado—to be conceited, or stuck up (usually as the direct result of some good fortune).

Ya que su jefe le ha dado un aumento de sueldo, está muy vitoqueado.
Now that his boss has given him a raise in salary, he's very stuck up.

Gastar pólvora en zamuros—to waste one's ammunition, or efforts on something not worthwhile.

No gastes pólvora en zamuros.

Don't waste your efforts on things that aren't worthwhile.

Hacerse el "musiú"—to deliberately change the subject; to play dumb (in the sense of avoiding the issue, or deliberately ignoring what's going on around you).

Cuando le pedí el dinero que me debía, se hizo el "musiú."

When I asked him for the money he owed me, he deliberately changed the subject.

Jubilarse—to play hooky.

(NOTE: This colloquialism is generally used in the PAST tense, with either PAST or PRESENT significance.)

María y Pedro se jubilaron.

Mary and Peter are playing hooky.

—or—

Mary and Peter played hooky.

(Also used in Guatemala)

Más es la bulla que la cabuya—Much ado about nothing.

PART VI

IDIOMS, EXPRESSIONS, ETC., PECULIAR TO SEVERAL SPANISH-AMERICAN REPUBLICS, *COLLECTIVELY*

PART VI

IDIOMS, EXPRESSIONS, ETC., PECULIAR TO SEVERAL SPANISH-AMERICAN REPUBLICS, *COLLECTIVELY:* **INCLUDING SOME OF THEIR MOST POPULAR COLLOQUIALISMS AND SLANG**

A. Central-American Idioms
B. South-American Idioms
C. Miscellaneous Idioms

A. CENTRAL-AMERICAN

Capear la escuela —or— **capearse**—to play hooky.

(NOTE: These two colloquialisms are generally used in the PAST tense, with either PAST or PRESENT significance.)

Capeó la escuela. —OR— Se capeó.

He's playing hooky.
    —or—
He played hooky.

(Used principally in El Salvador; also current in Guatemala and Nicaragua, Guatemala preferring *capearse*)

Darle chile—to tease one by making him, or her, jealous. (*applied to novios*)

Su novia le está dando chile.

His girl-friend is teasing him.
    —or—
His girl-friend is making him jealous.

(Used in Honduras, El Salvador and Guatemala)

[135]

Darse taco—to give oneself an air of importance.

Se da mucho taco.

He gives himself quite an air of importance.
(Used principally in Honduras; also current in Costa Rica and Mexico)

De quitá, quiero pasar—at the drop of a hat. (*fig.*); at the slightest provocation; for nothing.

Se enoja de quitá, quiero pasar.

He gets angry at the drop of a hat.
(Used in Nicaragua, Honduras, Guatemala and El Salvador)

Estar como gallina en patio ajeno—to feel out of place (at somebody's house, at a party, gathering, etc.).

Estoy como gallina en patio ajeno.

I feel out of place.
(Used in Costa Rica, Panama and Nicaragua)

Estar de alta con uno—to be in one's good graces; to be in good with one.

Estoy de alta con mi jefe.

I'm in good with my boss.
—or—
I'm in the good graces of my boss.
(Used in El Salvador, Guatemala, Honduras and Nicaragua)

Estar de goma—to have a hang-over.

Está de goma.

He has a hang-over.
(Used throughout all Central America, Panama preferring *tener goma*)

Estar en la lipidia—to be broke. (*finan.*)

Estamos en la lipidia.
We're broke.
> (Used throughout all Central America, principally in Panama)

Estar en las latas—*Same as above.*

Estoy en las latas.
I'm broke.
> (Used throughout all Central America. In Colombia: *estar en la lata*)

Estar socado—to be stewed, or three sheets to the wind. (*applied to an alcoholic condition*)

Está socado.
He's stewed. —or— He's three sheets to the wind.
> (Used principally in Costa Rica and Nicaragua; also current in Honduras, Guatemala and El Salvador)

Meterle (or pegarle) una yuca—to fib, or lie, to one; to tell one something that isn't true.

Me metió (pegó) una yuca.
He lied to me. —or— He told me something that wasn't true.
> (Used principally in Costa Rica; also current in Nicaragua and El Salvador)

No tener a quien volver a ver—to have nobody to turn to. (*fig.*)

No tengo a quien volver a ver.
I have nobody to turn to.
> (Used principally in Honduras; also current in Nicaragua, Costa Rica and Panama)

[137]

No tener ni petate en que caer muerto—not to have a penny to one's name.

No tiene ni petate en que caer muerto.

He hasn't a penny to his name.

(Used throughout all Central America. Also used in Mexico, where *caerse* is preferred to **caer**)

Quemarle la canilla—to cheat on, or be unfaithful to, one's husband.

Le está quemando la canilla.

She's cheating on him.

(Used in Guatemala, El Salvador, Honduras, and parts of Nicaragua)

Si gustos no hubiera, la jerga no se vendiera—Everyone to his own taste.

(Used in El Salvador, Nicaragua and Honduras)

Sobarle la leva—to polish the apple; to play up to one.

Me está sobando la leva.

He's polishing the apple.

—or—

He's playing up to me.

(Used principally in Costa Rica; also current in Honduras, Guatemala and El Salvador. In Nicaragua, the above colloquialism is more preferably rendered by using *cepillar a uno*)

Sobarle la varita—(1) to fire one from his job; to give one the axe; to can one. (2) to cut one off without any money; to cut off one's allowance.

(NOTE: More commonly used in *Sense #1*)

[138]

(1) Me sobaron la varita.
I was fired. —or— They canned me. —or— They gave me the axe.

(2) Mi papá me sobó la varita.
My Dad cut off my allowance.
(Used in Guatemala, El Salvador, Honduras, Nicaragua and Panama)

B. SOUTH-AMERICAN

(*Sp.*) **Estar hecho una uva**—to be lit, or three sheets to the wind. (*applied to an alcoholic condition*)

Está hecho una uva.
He's lit. —or— He's three sheets to the wind.
(Used principally in Ecuador; also current in Peru, Bolivia and Argentina)

Estar pato—to be broke. (*finan.*)

Estoy pato.
I'm broke.
(Used principally in Argentina; also current in Chile, Peru and Paraguay. In Uruguay: *andar* instead of **estar**)

Ir a la inglesa—to go Dutch treat.

Fuimos a la inglesa.
We went Dutch.
(Used in Peru, Bolivia and Argentina. Paraguay and Uruguay use *a lo inglés*)

¡La cosa quedó en agua de borrajas!—Nothing happened one way or the other! (indicating something being at a standstill, or failing to materialize)
(Used principally in Paraguay; also current in Uruguay and Argentina)

[139]

(*Sp.*) **Levantarse con el pie izquierdo**—to get up on the wrong side of the bed. (*fig.*)

Se levantó con el pie izquierdo.

He got up on the wrong side of the bed.
(Used principally in Paraguay; also current in Uruguay, Argentina, and parts of Chile)

Lo pasado, pisado—What's past is past. —or— Let bygones be bygones.
(Used in Argentina, Uruguay, Paraguay and Bolivia)

Pisar el palito—to fall into the trap. (*fig.*)

Pisó el palito.

He fell into the trap.
(Used in Argentina, Uruguay, Paraguay and Chile)

Planchar—(s.o. a girl when she is not invited to dance, at a party, gathering, etc. Hence, *to be a wallflower* —or— *to sit out every dance.*)

Planchó toda la noche.

She sat out every dance, the entire evening.
        —or—
She was a wallflower.
(Used in Bolivia, Chile and Argentina)

Sacarle pica—to deliberately annoy one; to tease one; to try to get one's goat.

Me saca pica.

He deliberately annoys me.
        —or—
He tries to get my goat.
(Used in Bolivia, Peru and Chile)

[140]

Se armó la de Dios es grande—All hell broke loose.
(Used in Chile, Argentina and Bolivia)

C. MISCELLANEOUS

(A) Cada muerte de obispo—Once in a blue moon.

(1) Used as a complete thought, as in the above phrase.

(2) Lo veo (a) cada muerte de obispo.
I see him once in a blue moon.
(Used in Argentina, Paraguay, Uruguay, Costa Rica and Panama)

A la muerte de un obispo—*Same as above*
(Used in Peru, Bolivia, Nicaragua, Honduras, and parts of Chile)

Allá donde el diablo perdió el poncho—Way out to Hell-'n'-gone.

(1) Used as a complete thought, as in the above phrase.

(2) Vive allá donde el diablo perdió el poncho.
He lives way out to Hell-'n'-gone.
(Used in Argentina, Uruguay, Chile, Bolivia, Peru and Ecuador. In Costa Rica: *chaqueta* instead of **poncho**)

Comer pavo—(s.o. a girl when she is not invited to dance, at a party, gathering, etc. Hence, *to be a wallflower* —or— *to sit out every dance.*)

Comió pavo toda la noche.
She sat out every dance, the entire evening.
—or—
She was a wallflower.
(Used in Guatemala, El Salvador, Honduras, Costa Rica, Panama, Ecuador, Cuba, Colombia and Venezuela)

[141]

(*Sp.*) **Dar coba**—to play up to one (giving him a lot of insincere flattery, etc.).

> (NOTE: This colloquialism is frequently applied to people in politics, or those who have a definite purpose in mind, such as, to gain a favor, to get into one's good graces, etc.)

Le da coba.

He gives him a lot of flattery.

> (Used principally in Cuba; also current in Mexico, Peru and Costa Rica)

Estar como perro en barrio ajeno—to feel out of place (at somebody's house, at a party, gathering, etc.).

Estoy como perro en barrio ajeno.

I feel out of place.

> (Used principally in Mexico; also current in Bolivia, Nicaragua, and some parts of Guatemala)

Gastar pólvora en gallinazo(s)—to waste one's ammunition, or efforts, on something not worthwhile.

No gastes pólvora en gallinazo(s).

Don't waste your efforts on things that aren't worthwhile.

> (Used in Panama, Colombia, Ecuador, Peru, Bolivia and Chile)

Pararle el macho—to stop one cold (in the sense of putting one in his place).

Le paré el macho.

I stopped him cold.

> (Used in Nicaragua, Costa Rica, Panama, Colombia, Ecuador and Peru)

(*Sp.*) **Se armó la de Dios es Cristo**—All hell broke loose.

> (Used principally in Peru; also current in Colombia, Guatemala, and in parts of Chile and Bolivia)

(*Sp.*) **Se armó la gorda**—*Same as above*
> (Used principally in Argentina; also current in Uruguay, Paraguay, Chile, Bolivia, Peru, Costa Rica, El Salvador, Guatemala, Mexico and Cuba)

Se armó la grande—*Same as above*
> (Used principally in Chile; also current in Argentina, Paraguay, Uruguay, Bolivia, Peru, Ecuador, Colombia, Venezuela, Panama, Costa Rica, El Salvador, Guatemala and Mexico)

(*Sp.*) **Ver los toros desde la barrera**—to view things from a distance (in the sense of not wanting to get mixed up in a fight, argument, etc.).

Veo los toros desde la barrera.

I view things from a distance.
> (Used in Mexico, Cuba, Guatemala, El Salvador, Nicaragua, Costa Rica, Panama, Colombia, Ecuador and Peru)

PART VII

BUSINESS IDIOMS AND PHRASES

PART VII

BUSINESS IDIOMS AND PHRASES

1° (primero) —*1st*
atta. (atenta) —*kind*
Núm. (número)—*No.; number; #*
ppdo. (próximo pasado)—*past; last; ult.*
afmos. amigos y Ss.Ss. (afectísimos amigos y seguros servidores)
　—*Very truly yours,*

A contar desde—beginning with; starting from.

A contar desde el 1° de octubre, le pagaremos $20.00 mensuales.
Starting from the 1st of October, we shall pay you $20 a month.

A la mayor brevedad posible—at one's earliest possible convenience.

Le agradeceré atienda el asunto a la mayor brevedad posible.
I shall be obliged if you will take care of the matter at your earliest possible convenience.

A quien corresponda (or **Al que le corresponda**)—To Whom it May Concern.

A razón de—at the rate of.

Teníamos treinta empleados a razón de $40.00 semanales.
We had thirty employees at the rate of $40.00 a week.

A saber—namely; to wit:

Puedo enviarle los siguientes artículos; a saber:
I can send you the following articles, to wit:

A vuelta de correo—by return mail.

Sírvase enviarnos, a vuelta de correo, dos ejemplares de su revista, "EL PORVENIR."
Please send us, by return mail, two copies of your magazine, "EL PORVENIR."

Abonar a uno en cuenta—to credit with; to credit to one's account.

Le hemos abonado en cuenta siete dólares.
We have credited seven dollars to your account.

Acusar recibo de—to acknowledge receipt of.

Acusamos recibo de su atta. carta.
We acknowledge receipt of your kind letter.

Al contado—for cash; on a cash basis.

Vendemos todas nuestras mercancías al contado.
We sell all our merchandise on a cash basis.

Al cuidado de—(in) care of.

Por lo pronto, sírvase escribirme al cuidado de la Compañía Editora Pérez.
For the time being, please write me (in) care of the Pérez Publishing Co.

[148]

Al fiado—on credit.

Nunca vendemos al fiado.
We never sell on credit.

Al por mayor—wholesale.

Nuestros libros los vendemos todos al por mayor.
We sell all our books wholesale.

Al por meñor—retail.

Esta casa no vende al por menor.
This firm does not sell retail.

Arrojar un saldo—to show a balance.

Su cuenta arroja un saldo de $52.19.
Your account shows a balance of $52.19.

Cargar a uno en cuenta—to charge to one's account.

Le hemos cargado en cuenta el importe de diez cajas de lápices Núm. 2.
We have charged to your account the price of ten boxes of #2 pencils.

Con carácter urgente—rush.

(1) Used as a label on packaged merchandise.
(2) Sírvase enviarnos, con carácter urgente, las mercancías ya citadas.
Please send us "rush" the above-mentioned merchandise.

Conforme a—in compliance with.

Conforme a sus deseos, le remitimos hoy 200 sacos de trigo.
In compliance with your wishes, we are sending you today 200 sacks of wheat.

Corresponder a uno (or **a la gentileza de uno**)—to return the favor.

Si puedo en cualquier ocasión corresponder a su gentileza, sepa que lo haré con sumo gusto.
If I can on any occasion return the favor, please know that I shall be very happy to do so.

(NOTE: In Spain, substitute *amabilidad* for **gentileza**.)

Dar anticipadas gracias—to thank in advance.

Dándoles anticipadas gracias por su cooperación, quedamos de ustedes, afmos. amigos y Ss.Ss.
Thanking you in advance for your cooperation, we remain, Very truly yours,

El actual—the present month; inst.

Su carta del 10 del actual.
Your letter of the 10th inst.

El corriente—the present month; inst.

Sirve la presente para acusar recibo de su atta. carta con fecha 12 del corriente.
This is to acknowledge receipt of your (kind) letter of the 12th of . . . (whatever this month is).

[150]

En lo sucesivo—hereafter; in the future.

Tenemos el gusto de anunciar que en lo sucesivo podremos proporcionarles toda clase de géneros.

We are happy to announce that hereafter we shall be able to furnish you with all kinds of materials.

Encontrarse en situación de *plus infinitive*—to be in a position to . . .

Nos encontramos en situación de poderles ofrecer un nuevo muestrario.

We are in a position to offer you a new line of samples.

Entablar negocios con—to establish business relations with; to enter into business with.

Hemos entablado negocios con la firma Gómez.

We have established business relations with the Gómez Company.

Está en nuestro poder—We are in receipt of . . .

Está en nuestro poder (Está en n/p) su atta. comunicación con fecha 26 de noviembre ppdo.

We are in receipt of your (kind) letter of November 26.

Estar a la par—to be at par.

Las acciones están a la par.

The stocks are at par.

Estar en el caso de *plus infinitive*—See: **Encontrarse en situación de.**

Hasta la fecha—up to now; up to date; up to the present (time); thus far.

Hasta la fecha no hemos recibido queja alguna de nuestros clientes.

Up to the present time we have not received any complaint from our clients.

Llegar a nuestro poder—to reach us.

Llegaron a nuestro poder (Llegaron a n/p) los cuatro ejemplares de su revista "AYER."

The four copies of your magazine, "AYER," have reached us.

Los corrientes—*See:* El corriente.

Obra en mi poder—I am in receipt of . . .

Obra en mi poder (Obra en m/p) su grata del 7 de diciembre ppdo.

I am in receipt of your (kind) letter of December 7.

Obra en nuestro poder—We are in receipt of . . .

Obra en nuestro poder (Obra en n/p) su atta. comunicación de fecha 18 de los corrientes.

We are in receipt of your (kind) letter of the 18th of this month.

Permitirse *plus infinitive*—to take the liberty of . . .

Nos permitimos ofrecerles nuestros servicios.

We take the liberty of offering you our services.

Poner en (su) conocimiento—to inform (you).

Tenemos el gusto de poner en su conocimiento que nuestra casa tiene un surtido amplio de tinteros.

We are happy to inform you that our firm has an ample supply of inkwells.

Por paquete postal—By Parcel Post.

(1) Used as a label in sending merchandise.
(2) Le he enviado hoy, por paquete postal, cien carteras para señoras.

I have sent you today, by parcel post, 100 ladies' hand-bags.

Por separado—under separate cover.

Le remitimos hoy, por separado, factura correspondiente al envío de 500 ejemplares de nuestra edición, "A THE-SAURUS OF SPANISH IDIOMS AND EVERY-DAY LANGUAGE."

We have today sent you, under separate cover, invoice covering shipment of 500 copies of our publication, "A THESAURUS OF SPANISH IDIOMS AND EVERY-DAY LAN-GUAGE."

Surtir un pedido—to fill an order.

Sentimos tener que participarle que no podremos surtir su pedido antes del 15 de los corrientes.

We are sorry to have to inform you that we shall not be able to fill your order before the 15th of this month.

Tener a la vista—to have before one; to have received.

Tengo a la vista su apreciable de fecha 21 de los corrientes.

I have before me yours of the 21st (inst.).

[153]

Tener en existencia—to have on hand; to have in stock.

Sírvanse avisarnos si tienen en existencia los géneros ya citados.
Please let us know if you have on hand the above-mentioned
goods.

Tenemos en nuestro poder—We are in receipt of . . .

Tenemos en nuestro poder (Tenemos en n/p) su grata de
fecha 2 de junio ppdo.
We are in receipt of your (kind) letter, dated June 2 (ult.).

Tengo en mi poder—I am in receipt of . . .

Tengo en mi poder su atta. carta del 8 del actual.
I am in receipt of your (kind) letter of the 8th of this month.

Verse en la imposibilidad de *plus infinitive*—to find it impossible to . . .

Nos vemos en la imposibilidad de aceptar estas condiciones.
We find it impossible to accept these conditions.

Verse en la necesidad de *plus infinitive*—to be compelled, or
obliged, to . . .

Nos vemos en la necesidad de rogarle se sirva remitirnos un
cheque por $16.75, para cubrir el importe de las mercancías
que le enviamos el 5 de abril ppdo.
We are obliged to request that you kindly send us a check for
$16.75, to cover the price of the merchandise we sent you the
5th of last April.

Verse en la obligación de *plus infinitive*—See: **Verse en la
necesidad de.**

Verse precisado a *plus infinitive*—See: **Verse en la obligación de**
—and—
Verse en la necesidad de

Zanjar una dificultad—to straighten out a difficulty.

Esperamos poder zanjar la dificultad a la mayor brevedad posible.

We hope to be able to straighten out this difficulty at our earliest possible convenience.